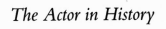

The Actor in History

The Actor in History

A Study in Shakespearean Stage Poetry

David Grene

The Pennsylvania State University Press
University Park and London

The quotations in this book have been taken from the *Riverside Shakespeare* (Boston: Houghton Mifflin Company, 1974).

Library of Congress Cataloging-in-Publication Data

Grene, David.
The actor in history.

Bibliography: p.
Includes index.
1. Shakespeare, William, 1564–1616—Knowledge—
Performing arts. 2. Acting in literature. 3. Theater in
literature. 4. History in literature. I. Title.
PR3034.G74 1988   822.383   87–43119
ISBN 0–271–00622–6

To Ethel and
Andrew and Gregory
with loving acknowledgment
of their loyalty and devotion

Contents

Acknowledgments

As lecturer for the Messenger Series at Cornell in 1978, I gave what is a recognizable version of this book, though it has been greatly amended and changed. I am grateful to all the kind people at Cornell, especially Sandra Siegel and Werner Dannhauser, who supported me in my visit to the University with appreciation and advice.

As I rewrote the lectures and gradually formed the book, I have been indebted to several friends and colleagues for useful discussions of the issues and for encouraging me to publish. I am especially grateful to Saul Bellow and Allan Bloom, to Wendy O'Flaherty, David Tracy, and A. K. Ramanujan. My former student, Professor Richard Garner, helped with the notes, Arthur Morey of Northwestern University with most valuable suggestions for revision, and Stephanie Nelson with her criticisms and very practical work on the final draft of a confusing manuscript.

As in everything I have written my greatest debt is to the many classes I have taught in the last twenty years under the auspices of the Committee on Social Thought.

Introduction

In this book I wanted to consider the relation which Shakespeare establishes between the values of the supreme world of Elizabethan and Jacobean reality, that of the kings and soldiers at the top of the tree, and his own domain, the poetry of the theater. Ostensibly, that poetry of the theater emphasizes straightforwardly the values of the plot of the play. By his poetry the king or soldier becomes more visible to us. We feel more compellingly his kingship, soldiership, because the rhythms of his voice, the verbal images and innuendos, reinforce the man and his acts as we see him in the regular story. Sometimes this is what happens. Henry V's famous speech before Harfleur ("Once more unto the breach, dear friends, once more" [*H5* III.1]) connects us forcibly with the excitement, tension, and glory of the moment of the battle, in its own terms—and Henry's terms. "Friends, Romans, countrymen," sometimes at least, strengthens our impression of Antony's passionate grief for the dead Caesar. But sometimes what takes place is different. Sometimes the poetry starting from a more shadowy identification of the character with his position in the story begins to substitute its independent or nearly independent values—its power to charm and to threaten and expand the "meaning" of the actor vis-à-vis his role. The character we watch on the stage escapes into an area where the sensations with which his acting affects us come also directly from his histrionic relation to us. He is more *actor, qua actor,* less actor of Brutus or Antony or Coriolanus. So Antony's "Sometimes we see a cloud that's dragonish" (*Ant.* IV.1.3) moves us by music and image to see the fragility of human individuality, as the actor can project it—not only or not chiefly as Antony can see or feel it. He so affects us because we know that the histrionic is a representation of the reality of emotion as definite and valid as impressionism is of the visual truth of the external world. What Shakespeare has done in certain of the history plays is to put at variance this, our sense of the histrionic, against the more usual values which we set upon political and military achievement.

Shakespearean histrionicism usually involves great richness and ambiguity of words and phrases in its dramatic expression—unlike Ibsen's haunted brevities and silences. When we listen to Antony and then to Octavian, we say: "Antony's world is an actor's world, but it covers more of the aspects of reality than Octavian's. I accept Antony's rather than Octavian's." The fantasy of Richard II is his escape from the harshness of the historical circumstances that belittle his capacity; clothed in poetry and growing into the actual presentation of the actor who rendered the part, it dominates us to the devaluing of the winner in the plot's completion.

My choice of the plays is personal, but, I hope, not very arbitrary. I have left out the three parts of *Henry VI,* and even the attractive *Richard III,* because the strength of the unified series *Richard II–Henry V* seemed, for my purpose, to supersede those earlier works dealing with the kings of England and the events of their reigns—because of the superior concentration that the later series possesses. I left out *King John* as hardly interesting enough and *Henry VIII* because of the problems of the joint authorship of Shakespeare and Fletcher.

Because I have sought to contrast what I have called Shakespeare's histrionicism most vividly with known historical deeds, as the raw material of the play, I have chosen those plays where Shakespeare has treated solid history for his subject; so I have chosen the chronicle plays, rather than those of prehistory or fiction like *Lear* and *Cymbeline* or *Macbeth*. Similarly on the classical side I have concentrated on the strictly historical Roman plays, such as *Coriolanus, Julius Caesar,* and *Antony and Cleopatra,* to the exclusion of the anachronistic *Troilus and Cressida* or *Timon of Athens.* Of course, even in the plays based on better-documented history, Shakespeare must invent tone, to some extent significance and emphasis, and even character, inside a given area of importance. But the importance is there already. The deposition and murder of Richard II, the conquest of France by Henry V, the murder of Julius Caesar, the victory of Octavian at Actium have an overwhelming actuality for a man of the late sixteenth and early seventeenth century. The dramatist is pressed for an interpretation of a pattern which is deeply there before he touches the story. Therefore the acknowledgment, indeed the superior stress on the actor's quality in the rendering of reality, is the more striking.

The order of the essays needs some explanation, as perhaps their entire interrelation. At first sight, *Antony and Cleopatra* seems misplaced. Why is it not with the Roman plays, and indeed in its dramatic position as a sequel to *Julius Caesar?* Why, since it is the most patent example of my theme, does it not bring up the rear of the essays as a grand climax? Why is its chronological place in the order of Shakespeare's writing disregarded, since it is the latest of the plays I have included? But these essays are hardly a reasoned discussion of a subject by successive arguments. They are rather, I hope, an effective sequence of images as the plays capture various aspects of the theatrical and histrionic in human reality, as human beings apprehend it. It is because I would have my readers more easily understand what I was talking about that I have put *Antony and Cleopatra* first. The hero and heroine almost consciously seek and explore the theatrical in their situation, and theirs is, in its effect upon the audience, a most brilliant, imaginative victory over the hard core of a more conventional reality which appears to overwhelm them. Their moment of victorious defeat lives in action, but action strengthened and transformed by the magnificence of poetry.

The histrionic in Antony is, truly, sometimes a feature of his defect of judgment, but in the play one cares less about the faltering of his good judgment, practically. We are too continually aware of the power of fantasy in both the protagonists, that power which has been created in each of them by their mutual passion. Antony and Cleopatra are, or were, hard-bitten realists. They would not accept for a moment the chance of failure if it were not that their love is driving them relentlessly, despite their moments of resistance from their former selves, to a new awareness of a different sort of victory, jointly shared.

Sometimes we understand their supreme moment through something more muted and ambiguous than the richness of poetry—in the harmony of an evocative simplicity of diction with a compelling emotion inherent in act or moment which conspicuously defies analysis. Why does Cleopatra's speech to Antony—"And welcome, welcome! Die when thou hast lived / Quicken with kissing. Had my lips that power, / Thus would I wear them out" (IV.15.38)—move us so extraordinarily? Because it goes along with the absurdities of a pretended struggle to hoist the heavy Antony up to the monument, as Cleopatra, too cowardly to descend, reaches to embrace him? The reaching of the woman's hands, the near recognition of the formalization of the lifting, the kiss itself fade into the longing and the cowardice. The words live half-way between a literal simplicity and the outrageous fantasy of "Had my lips that power, / Thus would I wear them out." This is the distillation of the histrionic in the *act*, which the poetry has seized and expressed. It works on us the audience as well as on the man and woman on the scene. That is why *Antony and Cleopatra* comes first in this short book—so that the reader may see first, in the perfectness of dramatic achievement, what the subject is which I have chosen.

For it is in a slightly different way, within *Richard II*, that the histrionic reveals itself: in the psychology of the man in whom it is native. We see how he experiences it, and how it hinders him practically, as it kindles his imagination. Richard has always been a dreamer; we become conscious of the changes in him, in how we judge him and dislike him, or judge him and still are carried away by what he makes us *see*. The conceit of the buckets full of tears (IV.1.181), the buckets which also symbolize his destiny and that of Bolingbroke, is intolerable in its aching self-pity and the grotesqueness of the combined metaphor. Yet it belongs in a continuum which climaxes in the tremendous abdication speech, which is perfect. In Richard, the emphasis always falls on the instability of mood, the back-and-forward of depth and truth and vanity and frivolity of the actor-by-choice. It explores a certain dimension of theatricality and instability in practical determination which is there in *Antony and Cleopatra*, but in that play not importantly, as of only one factor in the complexity of the action.

Richard comes before us as an actor, an amateur actor, so that it matters that we see both his imperfect shot at the sublime effort and his moments of perfection. In his role he is well suited, because he is a king (truly, I think, a sixteenth-century English king rather than one of his proper dramatic date) who is both himself and a nearly conscious actor of a role, the quasi-divine persona. This royal histrionic role he further transforms by fusing it with that of the Christus patiens.

Richard is inspired by theatrical reality; that is, he is keenly aware of a vision (shared with us his audience) of human reality which lives in images of voices, movement, personality of men and women, before us on the stage, speaking to our ears, challenging us by likeness and difference. He is inspired by the *sense* of this theatricality, and he is himself, somewhat uneasily, its conscious fabricator, as actor or poet. Not a little of the play is full of his dramatic posturizing, the preliminary exercises for his final dramatic triumph. The link between acting and kingship is vital in *Richard II* and the Henriad. We see it in its most explicit form in the contrast between Richard and Bolingbroke. Both are actors, for a king must be such, since the royal function is inseparable from acting. But the distinction between the two is between one who is an actor by choice, or weakness, depending on how you see the play, and the man who deliberately exploits his royal role to gain political ends, who puts off and on his part at the dictates of advantage or ambition.

In *Richard II* and the Henriad, decisive political power must rest in the hands of the king. He must be strong and resolute or the kingdom collapses into the anarchy of the warring nobles. The king may or may not be imaginative, that is, he may or may not see his position as an enlarged and vivid image of humanity rather than as a puzzle which demands solution. It would be fair to assume that either Hamlet or Fortinbras might be a competent monarch. But a dramatic imagination, mirroring in the actual stage presentation that amateur-actor quality in Richard II, is something special.

There lies the temptation to render the moment with an independence and inevitability just its own. Richard really disregards the necessity of a single choice, as for instance to fight for his crown or not to, because he explores avidly the emotions inherent in alternative courses both for our benefit and his own. So his natural inclination is constantly at loggerheads with political success, which is represented as lying in single-minded planning and ruthless execution of the plan.

But it is in *Richard II* that we begin to equate this political defect of Richard with a general sensitivity which is sympathetic to us as audience, which is constantly overextending itself to win our response, and which is in fact constantly blurring the difference between the actor whose profession it is to render the part for us and the character he represents within the mimic reality of the plot. Failure seems the price of this sensitivity, and, contrariwise, Bolingbroke comes before us as a man of interested hypocrisy and brutality and, above all, success. We are not at all surprised by his success or the final murder of Richard and his rival's repudiation of it.

For me, the two parts of *Henry IV* and, retrospectively, *Henry V* are dominated by the contrast of two sorts of drama. One is the contrivance of Prince Hal to play all his moves in the light of his final revelation as the proper Prince of Wales; the other is the spontaneous and genuine theatricality of Hotspur and Falstaff. Can anyone deny those moments of knowing that Hotspur is a more significant person than Hal? And, despite Hotspur's firm denials of any liking for poetry, isn't our admiration of him largely rooted in his immensely funny rendition of the battle scene starring the nobleman with the delicate nose? (*1H4* I.3.29) Isn't our sympathy for and love of Falstaff (and our discontent with Henry V's later discarding of him) tied up with the fictitious dialogue-reconstruction of the interview of Henry IV and his son? (*1H4* II.4.389)? Both of these impromptu renditions are humorous in effect. But the humor and the drama buttress one another and are used to reveal a level of sincerity, depth, and effectiveness of communication which undermines the stuffier values of the plot proper. Of course, it is the careless nobility of Hotspur, the comic vitality of Falstaff, which overwhelm us, and not simply the two scenes I have mentioned. But it is in those scenes that the two dangerous enemies of the Prince's future sober rulership define themselves, by the devastating power of mimicry and acting to challenge the solidity and seriousness of Hal's *contrived* drama, and indeed implicitly the importance of politics and history which are the materials of the plot.

In the Roman plays, *Julius Caesar* and *Coriolanus,* the tragedy again turns on the incompatibility of the political game with two of its chief players. Though the inner sources of the failure to cope seem different, the failure itself runs a predictably similar course. Both Brutus and Coriolanus go down because they have an inner vision which denies the value of winning by other people's rules. Brutus, if he is to be a leader, wants to lead a freed people to an old-fashioned Roman state, certainly never real in any historical era near his own and conceivably never real at all. Coriolanus wants to lead soldiers, in unending wars, under the banners and orders of an aristocratic Utopia. Both can only reject their contemporary world by adherence to a strongly prescriptive role which gives form to their ideals, and both find that form from their parentage. Brutus is trying to become his ancestor who drove out Tarquin, Coriolanus to become the perfect knight of his mother's dreams. Yet both move with all the passionate love of life filling the formal molds of their beliefs, and hating the insinuating fluidity of a winning pragmatism.

Both associate their inner certainty with glimpses of its theatrical aspects. Brutus sees the murder of Caesar as complete only when he sets the scene of the conspirators dipping their hands and swords in his blood, as the model for actors of the future (*JC* III.1.105); Coriolanus identifies himself as the winner of a new "title" as Rome's destroyer and, frustrated by his mother's intervention, says, "Like a dull actor now / I have forgot my part, and I am out, / Even to a full disgrace" (*Cor.* V.3.40).

Measure for Measure is in the book because of its mood and its structure. As I see the historical plays, in the chronicle and Roman versions, it can be a strange kind of commentary on them. The vision and fantasy of a particular man—a Richard II or Antony—confronts what the choric positions of the play assert as reality. The vision or fantasy is projected stagily, that is, in the stage trappings, the histrionicism, the slight exaggeration of theatricality which is the stage version of the dramatic itself. *Measure for Measure* plays with this staginess. But it plays with it in its relation to our active sympathy. For the activity of our sympathy implies a reality to evoke it, and it is with the nature of reality behind the sympathy and the theater that *Measure for Measure* deals.

The Duke's plans for Vienna and Angelo's acts are stagy. They arrive disarmingly into our minds as a sort of titillating melodrama. Not so the danger of death to Claudio and his reception of it, not so the complexity of feelings we see as existing between Isabella and Angelo. Angelo and the Duke, whose puppet Angelo is, belong to a political world where acts and counter acts can achieve any result, and factual reform and redemption work on every wrong. Such a political world and its management belong to fairy land. Tragedy, with another end superimposed, becomes comedy alternating in tone between verisimilitude and unconvincingness.

The rules of the theater *almost* obtain and are then perforated by arrowshots of doubt.

How does this comedy reflect our sense of reality as it lies behind our participation in the play? The comedy is very black humor. Let the corrective action be shown with all seeming gravity, what are to make of the legal distinction between Angelo the husband and Angelo the criminal when they have, between them, only one head to be chopped off? Or of the demands of a justice which can be satisfied by one of any number of heads—Claudio's or Barnardine's or Raguzine's? Or Isabella's pleading for Angelo's life, because he had only *wanted* to enjoy her against her will, whereas Claudio's penalty was just since he had actually lain with his woman to their mutual happiness? All these cases involve with mocking emphasis the winning out of what is inhuman, while logical in formulation. This is presented as the typical *legal* reasoning.

In the historical plays it is usually the man of subtler feeling, with words to match, who loses against his cruder and philistine rival. In *Measure for Measure* the matching is between acts themselves and the emotions involved in them, both translated into a kind of play-on-the-stage. Yet our sense of reality haunts us too as we watch the play; there is a recognizable appeal to our feelings directly—in the hatred Angelo awakens in us by his victimization of others, in the discomfort of our judgment on Isabella when her natural austerity finally joins forces with her indignation to provoke her open hatred of the brother she is supposed to wish to save, maybe finally in our ambiguous view of the Duke's bland maneuvers. More than anywhere else in Shakespeare, perhaps, we wonder what is the true commentary on a reality which reaches us so completely through a theatrical atmosphere. In *Measure for Measure* the reality which evokes sympathy is present as a conflict; between the facts, as they exist in an Alice-in-Wonderland law court—a fantastic archetype of the "real" world—and the tangle of emotion they awaken in us. The emotions part company with the story and yet retain some uncomfortable structural relation to it, leaving us full of pity, anger, laughter, and finally a mysterious sense of truth and correctness, the point of its application inexpressible. It is a play about ruler and rulership, about law and politics. But most, in its black comic mood, it is a unique study of the relationship of reality and the theater itself, the theater as the strongest expression of the personal awareness of reality, and its modifier.

A word about secondary sources. I have used only a few of these out of the many that were available; but I have used those that I thought especially relevant to my particular subject. Such books as I have quoted have mostly been written within the last thirty years, with the exception of some by Derek Traversi and Dover Wilson. I make my apologies to those who think that to do as I have done reflects an inadequate concern with professional English scholarship and so excludes me from constantly continuing arguments on points arising from the Shakespearean plays. Perhaps this is true. But I am not a professional English scholar but a strayed classicist, with a lifelong interest in theater from Aeschylus to Ibsen and Synge. If what I have talked about as my theme in this book is not interesting in itself to the general reader who shares my concern, it will certainly not become so through a more rigorous or complete citation of all those who have discussed anything like my subject already. It is solely to the uses of the intelligent general reader that these essays are dedicated.

❧ *1* ❧

Antony and Cleopatra:
The Triumph of Fantasy

*A*ntony and Cleopatra (unlike *Julius Caesar,* to which it
is a sequel) is only partly a political play; perhaps not
a political play even primarily, but a play of passion.
When Dryden called his version of it "All for Love: or the
world well lost," one feels the inappropriateness of the title
to the complexity of Shakespeare. But one thing that matters
is conveyed by Dryden's title—and is true when applied to
Shakespeare's play: that political power was lost by Antony
and Cleopatra in exchange for "something." The course of
our play describes "how" the power is lost. It also defines the
something that is gained. "Gained" is indeed not the right
word. In one sense there is no matching scale in which a
counterpoise for the empire is revealed. But Antony proves
right, for us the audience, when he says:

> Our dungy earth alike
> Feeds beast as man. The nobleness of life

Is to do thus, when such a mutual pair,
And such a twain can do't, in which I bind,
On pain of punishment the world to weet
We stand up peerless.

(*Ant.* I.1.35)

He proves right against the judgment of the other side, given by Philo's speech.

. . . you shall see in him
the triple pillar of the world transformed
Into a strumpet's fool.

(*Ant.* I.1.11)

The magic of the play bears on the reconciliation of the two statements: the nobleness of life in this instance involves the strumpet and the strumpet's fool in the chief roles. We, of the enchanted party, move throughout the play to a surrender to Antony's vision. But we so move against odds in the story, some aspects of the stage presentation, and some aspects of its main characters.[1]

For some, the moral issue has always been the decisive one. For them, the degradation of Antony, the historical setting of that degradation in the matching of the East against Rome, carries the emphasis of the play. Besides, probably the Jacobean audience hearing the words of Antony I have quoted here would have been struck by their wrongness and sinfulness. The identification of unlimited sensuality with the supreme value of life would offend a long and conscious tradition including both Plato and Christianity. Even some of the best modern critics of the play think that its greatest effects lie in the illumination of moral downfall and destruction.

For those of us who see it differently—as a revelation of

some new and positive value—the play has its own discomforts. The identification of Antony and Cleopatra as the necessary ingredient in the proposition "the nobleness of life is to do thus . . . when such a mutual pair and such a twain can do it" is where we begin to realize our discomfort. It is not an ordinary case of moralization, nor need we think ourselves prigs for being disgusted. There are certain shabby vices which are peculiarly disfiguring. If the play asserts the greatness of Antony and Cleopatra, what of the lies of Antony the politician as he makes a last effort to reestablish himself by marrying Octavia?

> Read not my blemishes in the world's report;
> I have not kept my square; but that to come
> Shall all be done by the rule.
>
> (*Ant.* II.3.5)

It is the seeming, almost-desperate sincerity of these words which makes us unusually disgusted by Antony's decision, taken within thirty lines, to leave Octavia. Even when one takes into account the impact of the soothsayer's words, it is hard not to call Antony's speech at some level sheer hypocrisy, and some sorts of hypocrisy are, in themselves, disfiguring.

What of the greatness of Cleopatra, tainted by her readiness to sell out Antony when he is declining and Octavian rising? (III.13.62–77). These are, it is true, only minor incidents. But there is such a lack of integrity (our notion of integrity) about them that we are at a loss to connect these people with a notion of human nobility.

Yet in the stage alchemy, Antony is proved right. In the play, the nobleness of life "to do thus" is especially true "when such a mutual pair," etc. Shakespeare has chosen a scene of political ruin and moral degradation to reveal this nobleness of life. The effect of the poetry is to convince us that here is true greatness, existing in a world exactly suited to bring out its meaning. What is created before us is a new poetic reality, which has subsumed the original story while freeing it from its obvious sordid implications.[2]

The power of words and rhythms, and the innuendoes lodged in their combination, substitutes for the sexuality of the predatory couple. This is true from the coarsest

> The mares would bear
> A soldier and his horse
> (*Ant.* III.7.6)

to the most transformed

> No more but e'en a woman and commanded
> By such poor passion as the maid that milks
> And does the meanest chares.
> (*Ant.* IV.15.72)

Bold tricks are played with the clumsiness in the stage presentation, or anticlimax in the mood, so that clarity or dignity in the moment of greatness is deliberately traded off for vitality. Antony tries to commit suicide—and fails; the actors make pretense of hoisting him up to the monument for his death scene (*Ant.* IV.15.32). Cleopatra induces his suicide—with knowledge or not, who will certainly say?—by a false story of her own death, lavishly embellished by Mardian (*Ant.* IV.13.27). Cleopatra gets the asps from the clown, whose black humor depends on his obsessional loquacity on his mission (*Ant.* V.2.240). This grotesqueness jars as the more explicit gravediggers' scene in *Hamlet* does not. Both the story and its staging lead us to believe that the tragic matching of reality and the dimensions of greatness or beauty imply a flawed reality. The spirit of the play might be summed up by what Enobarbus says about Cleopatra only:

> I saw her once
> Hop forty paces through the public street;
> And having lost her breath, she spoke, and
>   panted,
> That she did make defect perfection,
> And breathless, power breathe forth.
>
> (*Ant.* II.2.228)

The play ceases to be strictly itself—the passion of two middle-aged sovereigns who sacrifice their power to their love—and becomes an ecstasy in which the power of imagination has taken over the world and the world lives only in the power of imagination.

The play describes a man and woman who are past their moment of greatness and through their own weaknesses are losing out in a world of giant sharpers and gangsters, of birds of prey and their victims. This is Shakespeare's Roman world; his *Troilus and Cressida* shows a similar transformation of the scene of the *Iliad.* Among these vicious birds of prey Antony and Cleopatra had been as ruthless and unscrupulous as any; the will to be so, to top all the others, is still there. They are no longer in this supreme position of their ambition because they have met one another and the woman destroys the man. Not in the sense that Caesar destroys Pompey with the aid of Lepidus and destroys Lepidus. In that preying on one another the victor emerges as triumphant. Antony and Cleopatra in the relation cannot be predator and victim in the usual pattern. They are caught in a mutual passion which ruins their effective capacity for being himself or herself in their predatory roles. And so they perish, trying with increasing feebleness to be their former egotistic selves—Antony to dominate the Roman political world, Cleopatra to use her sexuality to secure an alliance with yet another successor to the imperial power.

The man is not even certainly brave anymore, except by fits and starts. He is sentimental, histrionic, a failure in any action with the tincture of the heroic about it, from fighting a battle to killing himself; no good as a politician, soldier, general. The woman is treacherous and silly, with no effective capacity for planning or even for understanding what is at stake in Antony's power game. But the poetry transforms the whole thing.[3] There is a glow about every scene which renders the hard surface of the plot—in the sense that I have described it—meaningless or insignificant. Our sense of greatness and our perception, our very understanding of greatness, arises from the identity of the magic words with the figure that utters them. Dramatic imitation of the figure is there; this is no lyric poem. But the imitation is nearly an original act in virtue of the effect of the poetry. Cleopatra in her death scene says:

> Give me my robe, put on my crown; I have
> Immortal longings in me; now no more
> The juice of Egypt's grape shall moist this lip.
> Yare, yare, good Iras; quick. Methinks I hear
> Antony call; I see him rouse himself
> to praise my noble act. I hear him mock
> The luck of Caesar, which the gods give men
> To excuse their after wrath. Husband, I come!
> Now to that name my courage prove my title!
> I am fire and air; my other elements
> I give to baser life.
>
> (*Ant.* V.2.281)

At this point we are barely aware that it is Cleopatra the pretended queen of Egypt dying. At least we are as little aware of it as is compatible with having come into a theater physically or mentally and seen an actor performing a continuous role for several hours. We are witnessing in complete participation some scene of mysterious balance between ecstatic joy in the defeat of death—and despair. In those words we see the greatness of the lovers in which we entirely believe because the poetry does not illuminate it; it is the greatness itself. The new poetic reality which has been created has swept together the outline of the story and its inner new infusion. It carries us to the point that our direct experience of the outside world—the part that bears on our sense of the play as imitation—is almost paralyzed.

This effect in its greatest intensity belongs only to the final scenes of the deaths of Antony and Cleopatra. But it has been prepared in the course of the play.[4] This, in its movement, conveys the illusion of development which in fact is our progress in imaginative response to poetry which is building to the climax of the revelation. In the first scene there are those two speeches which frame the area within which the movement takes place. One is Philo's:

> You shall see,
> The triple pillar of the world transformed
> Into a strumpet's fool.

The second is the speech of Antony already quoted:

> Our dungy earth alike
> Feeds beast as men . . .
> The nobleness of life is to do thus . . .

These are the two statements of the opposed meanings of the story that unfolds. In its course the speed grows slower and the rhythm stronger. The triviality and choppiness of the Alexandrian ladies-in-waiting, the dull catch-as-catch-can rhetoric of Octavian and his courtiers, the lameness alternating with brilliance of Antony's replies to the Roman charges against him, give place to the steady ground swell of the passion of the battle scenes and the suicides at the last. In the end, following the varying qualities of the poetry, we have come to accept the flaws of the characters and the flaws in the texture of greatness as theatrical truth—that is, as truth projected through the special medium of theatrical performance.[5]

Cleopatra's conversation with Dolabella after Antony's death is our clearest comment on the play's effect—the actualization of Antony's greatness, how we know and feel it. To achieve this, the poetry and the plot's presentation must take in and subordinate to its proper place the personal view of Antony taken by Cleopatra and Dolabella, and even the conventional assessment of his stature by his political and military rivals. These relative judgments must be seen for what they are and yet they must bear out, not qualify or diminish, the objective existence of that greatness. The matching of the poetry in the various views of Antony is a matching in quality: each piece bears on a certain dimension of the portrait. But it is not the ordinary completion of a portrait that is sought but a tally of all the emotions connected with it, arranged according to a certain hierarchy. Here is Cleopatra speaking her mind to Dolabella about Antony after his death:

> His legs bestrid the ocean; his rear'd arm
> Crested the world; his voice was propertied
> As all the tuned spheres, and that to friends;
> But when he meant to quail and shake the orb

He was as rattling thunder. For his bounty
There was no winter in't, an autumn it was
That grew the more by reaping. His delights
Were dolphin-like, they showed his back above
The element they liv'd in; in his livery
Walked crowns and crownets, realms and islands
    were
As plates dropped from his pocket.

Dol.   Cleopatra!
Cleo. Think you there was or might be such a man
        as this I dreamt of?
Dol.   Gentle madam, no.
Cleo. You lie up the hearing of the Gods!
        But if there be or ever were one such,
        it's past the size of dreaming. Nature wants stuff
        to vie strange forms with fancy; yet t'imagine
        an Antony were nature's piece 'gainst fancy
        condemning shadows quite.

                          (*Ant.* V.2.82)

We are made to feel the absolute sense of this miracle—
Antony's greatness—through the poetry. But the poetic
composition embraces his effect both on Dolabella, to whom
Cleopatra describes her sense of Antony's greatness, and on
Cleopatra herself. Each of these phases has the poetry appropriate to it to elicit our reaction on the scale. Each poetic
statement takes account of the limitation and distortion that
the special view imposes. Cleopatra's definition is indeed
overpowering; but it is related—insofar as it can be related to
anything concrete—to Antony's great political and military
past. She is doing just what he told her to do when he was
dying:

> The miserable change now at my end
> Lament nor sorrow at, but please your thoughts
> In feeding them with those my former fortunes
> Wherein I liv'd the greatest prince o' th' world,
> The noblest; and do now not basely die,
> Not cowardly put off my helmet to
> My countryman—a Roman by a Roman
> Valiantly vanquished.
>
> (*Ant.* IV.15.50)

But Cleopatra's tribute, in its wildness and grandeur, is moving us, against the background of our sense, not of his past glories but of the power and suggestiveness of the broken lights of greatness in his ruin. In that speech the dimension of her loss is as mighty as the explicit notion of past greatness to which she devotes her praise.

Enobarbus dies, overcome by Antony's generosity to him in his treacherous desertion. But what moves us is less this generosity, which so crushes Enobarbus, than its connection with Antony's explicit and humble avowal:

> Say that I wish he never find more cause
> To change a master. Oh! My fortunes have
> Corrupted honest men.
>
> (*Ant.* IV.5.15)

Enobarbus is the chorus in the piece—the chorus who mistakes because he proves untrue to his deepest self. Before he deserts Antony he provides us with the final worldly false assessment of the meaning of what we are watching:

> I see men's judgements are
> A parcel of their fortunes, and things outward

> Do draw the inward quality after them
> To suffer all alike.
>
> (*Ant.* III.13.31)

True; but his slightly later addition touches the other truth, in which he also shares:

> The loyalty well held to fools does make
> Our faith mere folly; yet he that can endure
> to follow with allegiance a fall'n lord
> Does conquer him that did his master conquer
> And earns a place i' the story.
>
> (*Ant.* III.13.42)

The identity of the "story," which I suppose is the true record of greatness, deliberately runs athwart the course of success and failure; it is the particular area belonging to the inward self of fatedness and choice which contradicts the self of calculation and judgment. That inward self is betrayed by Enobarbus, who in his last moment recognizes where the action had led him,

> But let the world rank me in register
> A master leaver and a fugitive.
>
> (*Ant.* IV.9.21)

The inward self Antony and Cleopatra increasingly recognize, both for sorrow and joy, despite superficial lapses to their older, more natural tendencies. There is indeed nothing entirely compelling for either of them except their mutual relation. After what he takes to be Cleopatra's desertion Antony says he "cannot hold his visible shape" any more than the clouds; Cleopatra, who always seems somewhat the better poet, says of Antony's death:

> The odds is gone
> And there is nothing left remarkable
> Beneath the visiting moon.
>
> (*Ant.* IV.15.66)

Octavian's funeral eulogy

> But yet let me lament
> With tears as sovereign as the blood of hearts,
> That thou my brother, my competitor
> In top of all design, my mate in empire,
> Friend and companion in the front of war,
> The arm of mine own body and the heart
> Where mine his thoughts did kindle, that our stars,
> Unreconciliable, should divide
> Our equalness to this
>
> (*Ant.* V.1.40)

is a good funeral eulogy as such things go; but it is Augustus's characteristically pursy and complacent voice that we can hear, and even his genuine tribute has been supplemented and in part superseded by our recollection of the wildly funny drunken scene when the drunken Antony dominated all the rest—and by the scene in which we hear Antony in conversation with the soothsayer acknowledge his feeling of despair when matched against Augustus as a rival for life's share of good luck.

Thus the play brings to us an impression of a man who is allegedly a great statesman and general, but whose true reality for us lies in the poetry written for him—in the words,

the rhythms, the enchantment. His poetic greatness super-
sedes the greatness of the public character in which he appears before us. The greatness of the poetry, his poetry and
that devoted to his portrait by others, dwarfs the conventional kind of greatness as shown in the story—the greatness
of military and political glory.[6] And his most telling poetry
belongs to the personal and inner man rather than to the public personality. This personal and inner man shows greatness
only in flashes, and often more in defeat than success; the rest
of the man's life may consist of a setting which is sordid
enough. The world itself, the total environment which together with the heroic character makes the possibility of
great and noble action, is itself, like that character, a com-
pound of glory and sordidness.

The truth to the imitated figure is still *just* there in this
stage personality. Antony still carries for us the aura of states-
manship and generalship. He is indeed like the remnants of a
politician and soldier, as Cleopatra is like the remnants of a
great queen and courtesan. Their mimed existence as great
public figures is kept before us but in muted terms; the passionate certainty of the poetry is reserved for the supremacy
of the greater reality and the greater greatness of their love
for each other, over everything else that they have done and
enjoyed. Here is where each one is truly poetically alive, and
therefore this is what we accept as being deeper and truer
than the rest.

The words and images which constitute this new reality,
when they express character, show mostly the deepening of
perception, rather than decision or courage or gallantry.

Antony, indeed, is a kind of hybrid caught between the
conventional greatness of his past and the talents that have
gone to make it and the awakening to the intensity of feeling
that could be evoked in him by the sensuality of Cleopatra—

the very qualities of the Egyptian which Philo and Octavian, sensibly enough, think have found out his vulnerability, his decline and corruption.

There is a great deal made in the play of the fallacy of Antony's choice. Octavian and his entourage—who stand to gain by Antony's weakness—are always afraid that he may suddenly show a new access of determination, change his mind and retrieve his Roman fortunes. But the kind of plot that Shakespeare is writing demands something other than choice. Voluntariness must be largely taken out of the situation; as something relatively trivial; it is the influence of necessity and fate that must emerge. When this has been allowed for, has indeed become part of the consciousness of audience and reader and the poetry still carries its power of transcendence, then and only then is the effect of the love affair properly triumphant in our minds. It must flourish in the midst of total defeat, and not a defeat that proceeds from Antony's choice of Cleopatra rather than Rome, rationally or heroically or romantically. It must proceed from an agony forced upon Antony. It is only then that the greatness acquires certainty of touch. It is only then that it is true.

There *is* in the play emphasis on the nature of choice, and of wrong choice—Antony poised between Cleopatra and Rome, Antony deciding between fighting by land or sea, Ventidius deciding whether or not to pursue his victory in Parthia. Yet it is the ominous undercurrent of necessity that we notice most—as far as Antony is concerned. Antony is middle-aged—is indeed very much the dying lion facing the lion's whelp. The soothsayer knows the truth—that Antony cannot match Octavian in competition. The music of the god Heracles who loves Antony tells the truth—that the god deserts him. The soothsayers tell the truth before the last battle. Political and military greatness is often represented as under fortune's control. The successful quality of a man like Octavian is that he rides the top of the wave, but that he does not try to steer too much by his own determination and intent. The offer of his sister Octavia to Antony in marriage is probably not the sinister act of statecraft that it is often represented to be—a sacrifice of someone he undoubtedly loves in order to have one more count against Antony. This indeed is the result. But the Shakespearean presentation of the successful politician—of which Octavian is an excellent example—shows him always just to the rear of a cynical awareness of his own acts. He plays it by ear, never consciously doing the unscrupulous thing that would confront him unmistakably with his own identity. This kind of practical knowledge is shown again in Menas's proposition to Sextus Pompey, when he offers to murder the Triumvirs aboard the ship. Pompey admits it would have been good service—but only if it had been done without his prior awareness.[7]

If Fortune is the vehicle of good for Octavian and his like, who wait for its currents, there is in both Antony and Cleopatra, at the end, the wish to discover something other than fortune to prove their greatness by, something that more clearly expresses that greatness as their own greatness. Antony's challenge to Augustus to single combat is made on the assumption that Augustus too would welcome such proof of his own excellence. Of course he does not:

> Let the old ruffian know
> I have many other ways to die
> (*Ant.* IV.1.5)

Because assuredly Octavian will go down, when Fortune finally turns against him (it never did historically), without any heroic effort to define himself against her. Cleopatra, with the same revelation as her lover has, is even more explicit; she says:

> My desolation does begin to make
> A better life. 'Tis paltry to be Caesar.
> Not being Fortune, he's but Fortune's knave,
> A minister of her will: and it is great
> To do that thing that ends all other deeds,
> Which shackles accidents, and bolts up change.
>
> (*Ant.* V.2.1)

For Cleopatra is as doomed and beyond the reach of safety arising from good counsel as Antony. It may be true of her, as Enobarbus says, that "age cannot wither her nor custom stale / Her infinite variety," but in Octavian she has met the successor to the Imperial purple who is not susceptible to her love charms. He is shown as wanting her in a grisly way for something very different—the humiliation and torture of his triumphal procession.[8]

The fatedness of the outcome, drawing on our (and the Jacobean) knowledge of classical history, rests on the old contest of East and West and on the historical survival of the unity of the Roman world for another few hundred years. For a short while it looks, within this play, as though there were a possibility of a division of the world between Alexandria and Rome, earlier, as later indeed it was to be divided between East and West in Rome and Byzantium. The marriage with Octavia is the would-be decisive step, an effort toward a unity based on a friendship which could not possibly last—as Octavian recognizes in his last speech over Antony's body. Within the play, then, the marriage of Antony and Octavia might have been the supreme example of choice, a choice that failed, because there was no will to follow it up.

Yet the emphasis is surely not exactly that. The marriage compact is only the last dying vestige of the old Antony the politician. It is the last time that he will put the temporal advantage, worldly benefit, Roman prestige ahead of his own realization that "in the East his pleasure lies." He makes the choice halfheartedly. The lies he tells are perfunctory and effusive despite their momentary sincerity. It is the verdict of the soothsayer, confirmed by the intuition of his own heart's superior truth, that takes him to the East.[9]

And so the givenness, the brute facts, is of the very core of the final scenes of greatness played by these two doomed lovers. It is exactly when they cannot fail to lose—but when they have tried to be their former selfish, efficient, sharp-witted selves—that their real greatness becomes incontestable in the poetry. Had Antony not made his last gesture as a Roman statesman by marrying Octavia and betraying Cleopatra; had Cleopatra not tried to betray Antony and save herself; had she not tricked Antony even if unwittingly to his death; had she not tried to make Seleucus lie for her; above all, had we not been left with just a shadow of doubt whether she might perhaps have chosen to survive if there had not been the certainty of Caesar's triumphal procession—by just so much would the overwhelming impression of the poetic reality of the pair been diminished, and their poetic greatness similarly impaired. The greatest moments of the revelation are perhaps Cleopatra's, and perhaps the greatest of these is the "I am fire and air" speech. But although it is the greatest of such moments, there are many more that almost challenge it, bearing on both the lovers and with just such difference in scale as suits the mood. Take, for instance, Antony's speech to Eros after he lost the battle and disgraced himself. He is on the point of receiving the false news of Cleopatra's suicide. He is a figure abjectly self-pitying and deceived. With-

out abating the reality, of the abjectness and self-pity—neither very heroic qualities—the scene gives us this:

> *Ant.*   Eros, thou yet beholdst me?
> *Eros.*   Ay, noble lord.
> *Ant.*   Sometimes we see a cloud that's dragonish:
>   a vapour sometime like a bear or lion,
>   a tower'd citadel, a pendant rock
>   a forked mountain, or blue promontory
>   with trees upon't, that nod unto the world
>   and mock our eyes with air; thou has seen these
>   signs;
>   they are black vesper's pageants.
> *Eros.*   Ay, my lord.
> *Ant.*   That which is now a horse, even with a thought,
>   the rack dislimns, and makes it indistinct
>   as water is in water.
> *Eros.*   It does my lord.
> *Ant.*   My good knave Eros, now thy captain is
>   even such a body; here I am Antony,
>   yet cannot hold this visible shape, my knave.
>   I made these wars for Egypt, and the Queen
>   whose heart I thought I had, for she had mine—
>   which, whilst it was mine, had annexed unto't
>   a million more (now lost)—she, Eros, has
>   pack'd cards with Caesar's and false-play'd my
>   glory
>   unto an enemy's triumph.
>
>   Nay, weep not, gentle Eros; there is left
>   ourselves to end ourselves.
>
> > (*Ant.* IV.14.1)

We may notice that it is Antony's mood of self-pity after
losing the battle which transforms itself into the universal

meaning of the loss of personal identity; but it attests the actual identity between himself as a man and the altering transformations of the clouds. As we have grasped that, we are then assailed by

> or blue promontory
> with trees upon it, that nod unto the world,
> and mock our eyes with air.

Those words in the extension of the metaphor have added a new and mysterious dimension to the comparison Antony has instituted and also to the emotion which makes Antony utter them.

In such a passage as this we have moved to somewhere where the excitement and joy are vested in the meaning of man's perception and his capacity to express it. Action is gradually being replaced by words which convey a richness of meaning impossible as long as the character and the situation, the pure mimetic constituents of theater, are sharply defining for what can be said.

Yet never has Shakespeare expressed, with such intensity of feeling as here, the last possible moment of union of an actual person in a world actually experienced, with the yearning to immerse the personality in a universal meaning; there is still here the credible unity of a person whose words can shift at will from the harsh, compelling, figurative

> that which is now a horse, even with a thought,
> the rack dislimns, and makes it indistinct
> as water is in water

to the overwhelming simplicity of

> the Queen
> whose heart I thought I had, for she had mine . . .

But we are now only a step to the last tragicomedies where character is only fleetingly present, where the plot exists in disjointed scenes put together almost like a scenario, and the words have taken over the whole area of emotional response.[10]

The mood of tragedy too has taken on strange bedfellows—grotesqueness, humor, deliberate and infinitely artful anticlimax—until it renders perfectly actual the combination of the last lingering glimpses of an ordinary world and the mystery of an enchanted meaning.

Much of this proceeds from an audacious readiness to play with the difficulties of stage presentation and the absurdities that it can create for passionate representation. The dramatist can make even theatrical limitations serve an artistic purpose. Look at the words here and the action that must accompany them. Cleopatra and her maids are at the monument—as the stage direction says, "aloft":

> *Enter* Antony *"below".*
>
> Ant. O quick, or I am gone.
> Cleo. Here's sport indeed! How heavy weighs my lord!
>   Our strength is all gone into heaviness,
>   that makes the weight. Had I great Juno's power
>   the strong-wing'd Mercury should fetch thee up
>   and set thee by Jove's side. Yet come a little—
>   wishers were ever fools—O, come, come, come;
>   and welcome, welcome! die when thou has lived;
>   quicken with kissing; had my lips that power,
>   thus would I wear them out.
>   (*Ant.* IV.15.31)

The effect is to join together the ridiculous effort involved in actors pretending to lift a heavy and fat man up a great distance and the rendering of poetry which for sheer transcendence of a human situation has never been equaled,

> quicken with kissing; had my lips that power,
> thus would I wear them out.

and the haunting music of

> I am dying, Egypt, dying:

The suggestion to the mind of the reader and onlooker is of a world created before him where human dignity, defeated by the physical need to lift the weight and by the need to be lifted, like a baby, joins absurdity and grotesqueness to its own quality, and emerges totally master of our minds and our love. Henceforth Antony's dramatic greatness is free of decisive humiliation in the story; for he has survived the deliberate humiliation of the observed action as the actor presented it—and there is no greater humiliation than this.

Shakespeare brings the very existence of stage and actors into the meaning of his tragic world. Cleopatra displays a superb contempt for the untruth of a mimicry which she is reenacting right in front of us—but with a difference.

> The quick comedians
> extemporally will stage us and present
> our Alexandrian revels. Antony
> shall be brought drunken forth, and I shall see
> some squeaking Cleopatra boy my greatness
> I' th' posture of a whore.
>
> (*Ant.* V.2.216)

We remember the drunken scenes on shipboard; we also remember Cleopatra's speech to Charmian.

> That time? O times!
> I laugh'd him out of patience; and that night
> I laugh'd him into patience; and next morn
> Ere the ninth hour, I drunk him to his bed;
> Then put my tires and mantles on him, whilst
> I wore his sword Philippan.
>
> *(Ant.* II.5.18)

And in the light of this, look at Cleopatra's very greatest speech:

> Give me my robe, put on my crown; I have
> immortal longings in me. Now no more
> the juice of Egypt's grape shall moist this lip.
> Yare, yare, good Iras, quick. Methinks I hear
> Antony call; I see him rouse himself
> to praise my noble act. I hear him mock
> the luck of Caesar which the gods give men
> to excuse their after wrath. Husband, I come!
> Now to that name my courage prove my title!
> I am fire and air; my other elements
> I give to baser life.
>
> *(Ant.* V.2.282)

Cleopatra's poetry of affirmation here is completely committed to drama—that is, to voice and body and listening audience. As one reads it or hears it read or sees it acted, one is supremely aware of the art of poetic theater. One sees the hint of personality, externally present in body and voice, and through this experiences the greatest things dramatic poetry can do in creating before us impersonal imaginative life. The queen is not only at her most queenly. She is also at her most actor-like.

As the lifting of Antony to the monument becomes part of the poetically real world where his greatness lives, so Cleopatra shows us the difference between acting, where only the obvious meaning of the acts is implied, and her own acting, where the poetry and the visible conduct of the actor have been fused into a new truth. Never on the stage has the daring and the mystery of acting been so demonstrated as in the last scene, that of Cleopatra's death. This actress, Cleopatra (played by a boy), can put the asp to her breast and say:

> Peace, peace!
> Dost thou not see my baby at my breast,
> that sucks the nurse asleep?
>
> (*Ant.* V.2.310)

❧ 2 ❧

Richard II:
The Actor in History

Several years ago I saw a much-praised performance of *Richard II* by the Royal Shakespeare Company. It was very clever and sensitive playing, concentrated on the psychological matching of the two competitors for the crown, the successful usurper Bolingbroke, Henry IV, and the royal failure—Richard II. As an audience we were often stirred to pity for Richard, perhaps even so to an appreciation of the play as a tragedy. But we were certainly given no hint of any affirmative theatrical value on the king's side; as far as those players were concerned he was a failure, and we were to see him as that.[1]

Such a rendering is unsatisfactory—because it does not do justice to the sense of exultation when one reads or, even more, hears read the poetry of Richard's past. Something is being established, on Richard's side, in one's consciousness, and it is not only pity; it is not the tragic sense either—at least not exclusively. Exultation it is; there is some winning by Richard, to match his losing, historically.

Fifty years after *Henry V* Marvell in his great poem on Charles I at his execution speaks of him as "the royal actor." This royal actor played the part assigned him by parliament but played it as that of the royal martyr. Is it possible that it is as the royal actor, in Marvell's sense, that we should see Shakespeare's Richard II—that his histrionic performance before our eyes is substituting for his sacred royalty, which is being lost to his incompetence as a monarch? There is no doubt of a certain lasting success historically on the part of Charles I. Whatever sort of ruler King Charles was, his performance at his death created an event which changed English political life for centuries, if not permanently.

In his British Academy lecture on Shakespeare in 1970, Philip Edwards presented an argument on person and office in Shakespeare's plays. Much of it is devoted to *Richard II*. In brief, Edwards holds that to interpret King Richard as an actor is to degrade him as king, and that Shakespeare and his audience would overwhelmingly support this distinction. As opposed to what Edwards sees as the frivolity of the acting part is the genuine fusion of person and office which he regards as Richard's condition.[2] "At his anointing the king is transformed; the change is final and cannot be reversed; the only way down is destruction."[3] He would thus establish *Richard II* as a tragedy; the king loses with his title his very identity, since his human person and his divine office are coextensive.

Every tragic play has a weight, an emphasis where it is at rest. This is where the feelings of the audience or reader are decisively engaged and united with the author's prepossession and purpose. Where is this emphasis in *Richard II? Is* it really in the defeat, in the "nothingness," once the king has lost his name and title? Or is it in what he is doing mentally with his destruction—with his poetic transformation before us, which is inseparable from the acting of the king by the king and the actor who represents him for us? Edwards wants to reject the idea of Richard as an actor because for him acting is to put on and off a role at will. This surely disregards how deeply in this play Shakespeare has rendered the art of acting—the relation of reality and the imaginative form given it by the player. It is indeed to accept Bolingbroke's division of reality and image when in mockery of Richard's shattering of the mirror he says,

> The shadow of your sorrow hath destroy'd
> The shadow of your face.
>
> (*R2* IV.1.292)

Does one reach out to this as the tragic truth, however cruel and however much uttered by an enemy? Almost certainly not. It is rather one of Bolingbroke's typical grossnesses, thoroughly jarring but not, in fact, satisfying us as to its truth.

Edwards rejects the idea of Richard as an actor because an actor suggests to him only the professional who plays a part written for him, and when it is finished becomes "himself" again. Bolingbroke is indeed such a one. Here he is as the popular prince—admittedly seen through Richard's hostile eyes.

> Off goes his bonnet to an oyster-wench;
> A brace of draymen bid God speed him well,
> And had the tribute of his supple knee,
> With "Thanks, my countrymen, my loving friends"

As were our England in reversion his,
And he our subjects' next degree in hope.

(*R2* I.4.31)

But King Richard is another kind of actor from that of Edwards's definition. First of all, he is an actor for whom no script is written—inside of the play we are watching. He is his own poet; the "self" that he finally creates is the role of the martyr king. This new self, in the process of becoming, is his acting part and is only understood by us, and by himself, in the process of improvisation. But it is an acting self and he is an actor because he is, inside of a story that calls for political decision, constantly responding to his own need to express in voice and body—most of all in "stage" words and phrases—a richness and complexity of emotion that only lives otherwise in the artificial setting of a theater.[4] For him there is always, somewhere, an audience calling for his chameleon transformations, demanding a Richard appropriate to his circumstances but so extravagant, eloquent, and versatile as no single character with direct genuineness could sustain.[5] The self-produced script is also supplemented by the knowledge on the part of both king and audience, of Christ's Passion (*R2* IV.1.237).

The vehicle of this new reality for Richard is royal martyr instead of ruler. But for the new character there is an additional inspiration, a kind of vague script drawn from the betrayal and suffering of Christ. Here is the outline of a role which is exactly suited to his imagination of himself and suffused by that imagination so that it becomes self-sustaining and originative. It becomes *his* myth, and he not only lives it but relives it. He is again Christ betrayed and suffering for his people. He discovers a new reality, an amalgam of himself and Christ as he experiences his final phase as Richard Plantagenet. In the ceremony of his abdication, which pretends to a legal formality for which there is no precedent, he gives this new reality its most complete expression.[6] Indeed he creates it. It is his original contribution to the transformation of his lost sanctity into a new awe—but rendered before us by the actor's art. He uses his actor self for it. The actor, playing him, acts his doing so.

Thus the first of this political series of plays is not only about politics. It is about two competing realities, the one based on facts and plans and stratagems, the other on something more personal, the fantastic and private acts of imagination. It is the latter that are transformed into stage terms. The imagination of Richard is calling for theater as a bridge between a mental construction strictly contained within his own head and some externalization that will take over and alter the hard surface of politics that had defeated him. The play he is acting is a dramatic progress from the old self, the ruler of England, to the new self, the martyr, with its functional climax in the abdication scene. There is a necessary fusion of the actor who is presenting Richard who is writing and acting the play for himself, loosely associated with his mythical pattern of Christ's suffering.

In virtue of our domination by the sound and the images which go to create the form and beauty of the poetry, we have embodied before us a kind of life richer than anything we have seen in his rival or even in the possibility of decisiveness and bravery in himself. When the theatrical illusion, in which Richard's speculations and gestures live so startlingly, makes us believe that here one has access to a deeper and truer reality than there, it is all up with the values of the less real. Yeats has described the effect of Richard's poetry in terms that ought never to be forgotten. He contrasts Richard II with Henry V later as reigning kings: "[I]nstead of that lyricism which rose out of Richard's mind like the jet of a fountain to fall again where it had risen, instead of that fantasy too enfolded in its own sincerity to make any thought the hour had need of, Shakespeare has given him [Henry V] a resounding rhetoric that moves men as a leading article does today."[7]

This play is not only about acting in relation to reality but about the actor. It is about a personality somewhere between a real professional actor—who is, of course, giving him substance before our eyes—and the man who in the world outside of the theater possesses the temperament of the actor, the temperament out of which the *art* of acting grows. The play shows us a process in which this histrionic man, Richard, is the chief figure in a historical process. Inside the play he makes a series of self-indulgent experiments in dramatic self-expression. The reception of the bad news from Ireland, as he receives it at Barkloughly Castle, incites him to the ready assumption of roles, of conqueror, of victim, of self-discovered imposter—mere man, no king.

Here we get our first glimpse of Richard as the man who uses images with the evident intention of substituting fantasy for action. It is a prolonged series of images at first worked out on the assumption of a victory effortlessly achieved, achieved through the assumed inherent power of the images. He enlists the earth and her noxious beasts in the service of the king against Bolingbroke.

> Dear earth, I do salute thee with my hand . . .
> Feed not thy sovereign's foe, my gentle earth,
> But let thy spiders, that suck up thy venom,
> And heavy-gaited toads lie in his way . . .
>
> (*R2* III.2.6)

Then comes the analogy of the king and the sun, and the ability of the sun to defeat darkness and its shelter for rebels. Finally Richard speaks triumphantly of the sanctity of the king which overrides any earthly power. These statements are clearly not to the taste of the strongest minded of his followers, to judge from the implications of his own remark, "Mock not my *senseless* conjuration, lords," and the Bishop of Carlisle's gentle rebuke,

> The means that heavens yield must be embrac'd,
> And not neglected; else if heaven would,
> And we will not. Heaven's offer we refuse,
> The proffered means of succor and redress.
>
> > (*R2* III.2.29)

We are reminded here that Richard's long speeches all live in a special histrionic situation, in which he is constantly in danger of losing the sympathy of his immediate audience. His is a special kind of acting, full of musing, soliloquy, generalization. The actor who played Richard must have shown the king as thinking like a poet, playing like an actor who is constantly escaping his immediate audience, in the play itself to a more general one—that is, the audience before him in the theater—and all in a story which emphasized the values of power and revolution. There is thus an obvious comparison implied and at times expressed between realism and acting, to the disadvantage of the latter—as far as the play's story goes. Reflective, introspective, the king reaches out too eagerly to impress his own construction on the intractable mass of circumstance. Despite the greatness of much of the poetry in the scene at Barkloughly Castle, it is still suffused by Richard's weakness, the need too closely to express *himself* and his dilemma. When later we come to the abdication scene, the agony of the king has created a ceremony which is devoid of this smallness of the man who performs it.

In act III, scene 2, we started with images derived from the prospects of victory. But we move on, and can feel the delight with which he improvises a different role for himself, based on defeat:

> Mine ear is open, and my heart prepar'd.
> The worst is worldly loss thou canst unfold.
> Say, is my kingdom lost? Why 'twas my care.
> And what loss is it to be rid of care?
> Strives Bolingbroke to be as great as we?
> Greater he shall not be. If he serve God,
> We'll serve him, too, and be his fellow so.
>
> (*R2* III.2.92)

Finally in the end of one of his greatest dialogues with himself and his audience ("For God's sake, let us sit upon the ground, / and tell sad stories of the death of kings"), Richard suggests a new "reality" which explicitly denies the sacred kingship which underlies all his previous assumptions; suggests that if such a kingship is separated from its outward forms and resources it does not exist:

> Cover your heads, and mock not flesh and blood
> With solemn reverence, throw away respect,
> Tradition, form, and ceremonious duty,
> For you have but mistook me all this while:
> I live with bread like you, feel want,
> Taste grief, need friends: subjected thus,
> How can you say to me I am a king?
>
> (*R2* III.2.171)

Roles so easily assumed take over all the chances and inco-
herences of real life. Indeed, as we see in the last passage, they
can undermine the very foundation of the moral universe as
previously understood. The versatility of Richard in this regard starts to break down all differences between the external
world and mental constructions. It is noteworthy that Bolingbroke earlier in the play has rejected for himself any such
attitude.[8] His father, John of Gaunt, had advised him to
soften his sentence of exile by the fiction:

> Think not the King did banish thee
> But thou the King . . .
>
> *(R2* I.3.279)

To which Bolingbroke answers:

> O, who can hold a fire in his hand
> By thinking on the frosty Caucasus?
> Or cloy the hungry edge of appetite
> By bare imagination of a feast?
>
> *(R2* I.3.294)

Bolingbroke never loses the sense of reality which provokes him to action and redress; Richard is never free of the
temptation to turn everything external into a play which he
directs with himself in the main role.[9] But Richard neither in
his character nor in the extraordinary poetry that expresses
it—both centered in a self-conscious extravagance and in-
ventiveness—leaves us with clear judgment against the self-
indulgent and incompetent amateur actor. The discomfort of
the reality of the defeat, as it looms larger and finally overwhelms him, neither generates in us a moral conviction
against him, nor does it stop at making us pity him. Instead

there is a mysterious power in his stage performance which makes us partly see a self-deluded man of eloquence—but also half see another reality being created by theatrical art in which Richard is not conquered but conqueror.

There is another passage in which we still see Richard ineffectually using his histrionic gift to combat his sense of royal failure. In the image of the two buckets, Richard half-consciously plays with his grief in mannered coyness, almost to bathos. The poetry tantalizes us, between resentment at the posturing and mesmerization at the skill.

> Here, cousin, seize the crown.
> Here, cousin,
> On this side my hand, and on that side thine
> Now is this golden crown like a deep well
> That owes two buckets, filling one another,
> The emptier ever dancing in the air,
> The other down, unseen, and full of water.
> That bucket down and full of tears am I,
> Drinking my griefs, whilst you mount up on
>   high.
>
> (*R2* IV.1.181)

But we are led on to the climax of the deposition scene when the invented abdication ceremony, the shattering of the mirror, in its theatricality has created a true dramatic event which takes over and overcomes the obvious meaning of the story which is his total defeat[10]—with no mean sense of self-pity to mar it. After that, the death scene in Pomfret, and especially the speech "I have been studying how I may compare," is indeed pathos, an anticlimax to the glory of the deposition, ending as it does in the struggle with the jailer and murderers. I cannot see how it can be construed in any other way.

With Edwards's interpretation of Richard as titleless prince,
yet still holy, his death must surely bear the chief weight; yet
it seems to me that it certainly does not.

All three kings of this chronicle series—Richard II, Henry
IV, and Henry V—are actors, of a sort. They have to be,
since the king as representative of his nation, if nothing else,
is a kind of actor. Richard is the only one of the three that is
naturally and joyfully an actor. He is the one who reveals to
us what acting is all about. I believe that Shakespeare saw
the contemporary king as suggestively similar to the actor in
his relation to his role, where that relationship is deepest—
where the role is something that grows from himself and yet
is not identical with himself, nor yet quite consciously controlled by his will; where the self is expansible; where indeed
the new self is only understood in the process of representation. Richard knows, in a mood between conscious reflection
and intuitive feeling, the truth that inheres in acting—in the
emotional surrender to a preconceived pattern of fictive passion. He is unquestionably supported in this by the remem-
brance of Christ's suffering, though he mentions this only in
the abdication scene. We follow him through a hit-and-miss
human progress of expression, mostly stirred by his least
agreeable qualities—his self-pity, weakness, hysteria—to a
genuine artistic triumph, in the abdication. This artistic
triumph is the demonstration before our eyes of how stage
poetry creates its version of truth—in this case the role of
royal martyr. It is a *moment* of truth only.

In *Richard II* Shakespeare reflected on the kind of man that
is naturally an actor, and how effective such a one will be as
a politician. This man has the histrionic temperament; he sees
the world as dramatist and actor. For Shakespeare here the
two are almost the same. He has drawn together this actor's
gift with the character most likely to possess it—a man

imaginative, introspective, self-indulgent, and incompetent, with too much appetite for emotion and not enough determination to guide any practical course of action. There is in him all the good and the bad to be expected, the melodramatic posturer and the true actor. Through the degradation of his self-pity he rises to the true creation of the supreme moment of the play, in the abdication. It is not too much to say that here, in its associated images, the actor captures the numinal quality which replaces the fiction of the king's traditional royal self—but now attached to martyrdom.

It is a moment only. The moment is part of a lifetime, and the amateur dramatist is mostly unfitted to the political existence in which he must function. In the first play of the series (*Richard II–Henry V*) begins a contrast between such a temperament, which is less a character itself than a vital mood and configuration of man's thought, with the simpler "this is real," "that is acting," "we win," "we lose" of the historical account on which the play is based. In the later plays, Hotspur and Falstaff, in quite different ways, constitute a theatrical challenge to the values of history and politics. Thus the whole series, starting with the failure of the royal histrio to cope with the successful Bolingbroke, becomes a sort of competition between dramatic emotion and the achievements of war and statecraft.

It is not that the poetry of Richard's part positively asserts the truth of the mind's life against the solid facts of historical events. It only hints this. It is that the mind's life, represented by a man who is a practical failure, has a subtlety of quality which balances or almost balances the defeat. Richard is a dramatic poet with an extraordinary creativeness which he demonstrates before our eyes. At the very least this invests the defeat with a meaning which is upsetting and which disrupts any simple judgment between the king and the usurper;

at its greatest, Richard's poetry conveys to us a passionate reality which can never henceforth be dismissed in the next three plays.[11] In this sense Richard never ceases to haunt his successors, and our response to him, reawakened by the other two eloquent failures, Hotspur and Falstaff, tends to set at odds the direct meaning of the history and the emotion awakened by the poetic fabric.

For Richard it is the real facts of revolt, desertion, and his own imminent deposition and death which stimulate him. But they stimulate him not to counter-action but to a form of counter-creation in images and words—to the image of the buckets; to the abdication ceremony, and to the shattering of the mirror. These images, by their poetic force, situated in the passion of the king's martyrdom, wrest the brute facts from their conventional meaning and invest them with another which is, or appears to be in the moment, truer to some final human reality. The glimpse of this reality is the more convincing because we have followed Richard through several scenes and several great speeches which are similar but too personal. They show us the kind of man and the kind of histrionics he is inclined to—yet they do not blur the authenticity of the truly artistic scene of the abdication, when it comes, and the shattering of the mirror.

These early moments of histrionic possession, and their speeches, create before us near-tragedy, marred by Richard's self-pity. But with all the back and forth of human imperfection, the king rises decisively to the poetry of his great scene dominating Bolingbroke and his followers. Here the self-pitying Richard, the hysterical Richard, the unjust and cowardly Richard are all gone. The poetry here is almost unmediated by the particular character that utters it; it is tinged with the role of martyr, but in general terms. The pseudo-legal cadences and formulations translate the abdication into a ceremony of pure magic; the shattering of the mirror is indeed the final act of the new drama in the breaking of the king's image in the glass.

Despite some superficial similarities to the earlier chronicles, the structure of *Richard II* is something very innovative indeed. The play groups itself into several great movements. The first deals with Richard's incompetence and viciousness as king and politician. It covers the Mowbray-Bolingbroke quarrel, Gaunt's death scene and the seizure of his property. The temporizing on Bolingbroke's sentence, perhaps altogether the inequality of the two punishments, and the half-explicit references to Gloucester's death, above all the patent insecurity of Richard's demand for a pledge from both rebels that they will not combine forces, all give, in concentrated form, the reasons why Richard will not be able to be an effective ruler for long. In this context Richard shows, as well as his personal weaknesses, the generic situation of the "new" despot. The nobles are constantly on the watch for the chance to replace an unpopular ruler by someone more acceptable to themselves, provided he is closely related to the deposed monarch. We must remember the chronicle tradition that Richard is a centralizing ruler; this view has recently been endorsed by Professor Elton, who sees the historical Richard's downfall as due to the action of the remnants of a feudal nobility.[12] Such a centralizing despot is also traditionally accused of seizing his subjects' property unlawfully.

But certainly the Mowbray-Bolingbroke quarrel and the John of Gaunt scenes are used simply as massive examples. The step-by-step progress in the king's ruin after that, which we would expect, on the model of the earlier chronicle plays, is not followed out at all. The collapse of the king's power (act II, scene 2) contrasted with Bolingbroke's success (scenes 3 and 4) is treated sketchily and slightly. At act III, scene 2, we settle down to the weight of the play, which is the impact on Richard, as man and king, of his impending destruction. The whole strength of this play is closely connected with the way in which the struggle has been changed from a contest between Richard and Bolingbroke to the contrast in tone and meaning of the conflicting forces in the king's mind.

Let us now examine briefly the three great movements of the play in three speeches: first, Richard's failure as ruler; second, his triumph as a martyr; third, his epilogue facing death. The first of Richard's three great speeches is:

> For God's sake let us sit upon the ground,
> And tell sad stories of the death of kings;
> How some have been depos'd, some slain in war,
> Some haunted by the ghosts they have deposed,
> Some poisoned by their wives, some sleeping kill'd,
> All murthered—for within the hollow crown
> That rounds the moral temples of the king,
> Keeps Death his court, and there the antic sits,
> Scoffing his state and grinning at his pomp,
> Allowing him a breath, a little scene,
> To monarchize, be fear'd and kill with looks,
> Infusing him with self and vain conceit
> As if this flesh which walls about our life
> Were brass impregnable; and humor'd thus,
> Comes at the last and with a little pin
> Bores through his castle wall, and farewell king!
>
> (*R2* III.2.154)

What comes across here is an actor's presentation, from the inside, of a tragic role. The emotion which the role awakens is shared by the spectators and by the king himself. The fates of England's kings, past and to come, are drawn toward his own. Yet there is here no special personal relevance that he discovers; only the common ironical absurdity of the monarch, before God and man, which tempts the king to see himself double, as the man that is and the Divine Servant that may be, but who is nonetheless, even with his Divine support, as susceptible to poison, the dagger, treachery, as anyone else.

Our feeling for this passage depends on letting go of a sharp definition of the character of Richard II and yielding ourselves to his vision of man's folly of grafting on mortality the concept of eternity and the visible attributes of God.

Richard presents his part as a universal claim for pity for mankind, in man's delusive claims to transcendent meaning. We are not asked to see this as Richard's reaction to his own impracticality. It grows out of Richard's character, but that character is itself general in outline. It stems from a mind that somewhat easily associates its own fate with what Yeats called "the chimeras that haunt the edge of trance."[13] Those dead, killed kings are there in the form of a spell. "Some" . . . "some" . . . "some" . . . echo so exhaustively that the categories seem more inevitable than any other assertion of fate will be; the abrupt stop, "all murdered," leads to the conclusion in the absoluteness of Death as "antic" and "scoffer" with his little pin effective against the walls of brass. This spell is neither characteristic of Richard as a man nor yet quite divorced from that histrionic weakness of his as contrasted with Bolingbroke's activity. It is the real territory of stage poetry where the universal is held—momentarily and uncertainly—within the capacity of a single mind, a single voice and a single body, to express.

The poetry of the first of these three speeches of Richard's emphasizes the illusion of the monarch as a ritualized object when confronted with his own human vulnerability. Now the poetry of the abdication speech throws the weight the other way. It too is histrionic poetry—that is, poetry bred of the almost conscious association of the show of acting with the man the role is supposed to represent:

> With mine own tears I wash away my balm
> With mine own hands I give away my crown
> With mine own tongue deny my sacred state
> With mine own breath release all duteous oaths
> All pomp and majesty I do foreswear;
> My manors, rents, revenues, I forego;
> My acts, decrees and statues I deny;
> God pardon all oaths that are broke to me!
> God keep all vows unbroke are made to thee!
> Make me, that nothing have, with nothing
>   griev'd,
> And thou with all pleas'd, that have all achiev'd!
> Long mayst thou live in Richard's seat to sit,
> And soon lie Richard in an earthy pit . . .
> God save King Henry, unking'd Richard says,
> And send him many years of sunshine days.
>
> (*R2* IV.1.207)

Here the effect of the ceremonial repetitions and the skillful rhythmical imitations of legal phrases go to assure us that what man believes about the king is true—that he is God-created and supported and that only to God is he accountable. What we see is a king sacrificing himself, by withdrawing himself from God's protection as he abdicates the task to which, he thinks, God no longer finds him suited. Finally under goading of Northumberland to read a record of his offenses for the benefit of the Commons, Richard demands instead a mirror.

Give me that glass, and therein will I read.
No deeper wrinkles yet? Hath sorrow struck
So many blows upon this face of mine
and made no deeper wounds? O flatt'ring glass,
like to my followers in prosperity
thou dost beguile me! Was this face the face
that every day under his household roof
Did keep ten thousand men? Was this the face,
That like the sun, did make beholders wink?
Was this the face which fac'd so many follies,
And was at last outfaced by Bolingbroke?
A brittle glory shineth in this face.
As brittle as the glory is the face
For there it is, cracked in a thousand shivers.
Mark, silent king, the moral of this sport
How soon my sorrow hath destroy'd my face!
                                        (*R2* IV.1.276)

Richard is outraged because he finds that his person and his
office are not coterminous—as should be the case in a medie-
val monarch. He sees they are not coterminous in that peculiar, whimsical, affected vein in which nearly all his most in-
timate thoughts are couched, because his face does not show
the wounds which the loss of his crown has inflicted. He
breaks the glass as an act of judicial revenge against the man
who ruined the king—that is, himself. The shattering of the
glass shocks us into seeing Richard himself annihilating the
king-person, a kind of suicide which is a logical last step after
the equation of the image of the full and empty bucket with
the twin rivals, and the abdication of Richard from his office.
The mirror as object is especially effective because the king-
person exists, as far as the rest of mankind goes, largely
through images. Men know that in the king they are not

seeing reality literally in the king's divine-human relation. The breaking of the glass expresses perfectly the literalness of the event and the mysterious import of the symbol.

But a new element has been added to the scene which frames the abdication. Before it gets under way, when Richard is led in to be asked to make the declaration for the Commons, which he refuses, and before he rises to the heights of his strange, inspired ritual moment, he says:

> Give sorrow leave a while to tutor me
> To this submission! Yet I well remember
> The favours of these men. Were they not mine?
> Did they not sometimes cry "All hail!" to me?
> So Judas did to Christ; but He in twelve
> Found truth in all but one: I in twelve thousand,
>   none.
>
>   (*R2* IV.1.166)

Richard is finding his supporting script. He is finding the fragments of the myth, the outline to carry his purified emotion through the scene he is about to act—and create. He is Christian in the holiness which is violated—but he is particularly Christ in the infidelity around him. The last dregs of his self-pity ebb away in the sentence on Judas. He is free to be the actor for the greatness of his part, with the necessary impersonality which its legalism and formal structure call for.

What Richard has done is to re-create the "reality" which lies behind Bolingbroke's "shadow." Here is the poetic version of legalism, where the legal phraseology, instead of tightening the security of the contract, goes to deepen the meaning of Richard's personal destruction and give it a new emotional dimension. The decisive moment is the abdication and abjuration of his office.

As he has finished his long renunciation of his powers and titles, he has this to say:

> Nay, all of you that stand and look upon me
> Whilst that my wretchedness both bait myself,
> Though some of you, with Pilate, wash your hands
> Showing an outward pity, yet you Pilates
> Have here delivered me to my sour cross,
> And water cannot wash away your sin.
>
> > (*R2* IV.1.237)

In "bait myself" there is his inward sense of failure and humiliation, but in the identification of the other actors as Pilates there is the other element of the myth. He is indeed the Christ as Richard, and his abdication has become his crucifixion. It is his own invented gesture which supplies the original act substituted for the Passion.

Yet he is a new Christ, one who knows that he baits himself as well as being sacrificed by the sour Pilates. It is a new humanity intruded into the Christ figure, the sacrifice unrelieved by the certainty of divinity which sustains the Christ. This concluding touch reminds us of the dual quality of acting: part of Richard's suffering is deliberately self-inflicted. He *seeks* the misery that can be transferred into the histrionic. But then the role of his myth comes to his rescue and he can see, in his final act of self-identification, his audience, as the accomplices in his objective destruction.

Yet it is not only the sacrifice itself that moves us. It is the strange solemnity with which this ritual evolves before our eyes. We see how a king is unmade. The illusion of ceremony takes over reality so that we seem to participate in some orig-

inal act where God shifts his support from one Servant to
another; it is the words of Richard which perform this act.
The words that enact the spell have become almost impersonal in their validity. They no longer stem from Richard the
failure or exclusively from Richard the martyr. They constitute a living force which produces a result which is immediately apparent.

In the third of Richard's great scenes one comes on another
aspect of the relation of actor and king. Here Richard, having
abdicated, and facing death in his cell, relives his past with
the freedom of one to whom it is now only material for a
play:

> I have been studying how I may compare
> This prison where I live unto the world;
> And for because the world is populous,
> And here is not a creature but myself,
> I cannot do it; yet I'll hammer it out.
>
> My brain I'll prove the female to my soul,
> My soul the father, and these two beget
> A generation of still-breeding thoughts;
> And these same thoughts people this little world,
> In humours like the people of this world;
> For no thought is contented . . .
>
> Thus play I in one person many people
> And none contented: sometimes am I king,
> Then treasons make me wish myself a beggar,
> And so I am. Then crushing penury
> Persuades me I was better when a king,
> Then am I king'd again, and by and by,
>
> Think that I am unking'd by Bolingbroke,
> And straight am nothing. But whate'er I be,

> No I nor any man that but man is,
> With nothing shall be pleased, till he be eas'd,
> With being nothing.
>
> (*R2* V.5.1)

For Shakespeare's Richard, reflection on the past is an imaginative reconstruction in which that past is given what turn he chose it should have had, and his part in it is changed accordingly. It is always in the form of a play which he rewrites and then plays. Always the rewriting is demanded by the distaste which is the result of playing one version of the play to a conclusion. But this is now a play without an audience—and an actor must have one. In the end, the imagination itself wearies without more tangible evidence of real people. And so Richard sees death as the last alternative to his aimless, unceasing replaying of the roles.

Richard in his own mind is God's Servant; but he is also a vulnerable man. The combination of the two, in the mystery of a single being, belongs with full realization of himself only in his sorrow and fall. It is as though being God's servant permitted him an area where real humiliation and suffering yielded to the joy of performing a part foreordained for him. In this shadowy country, the king can observe somebody being created with his voice and his words, but neither himself nor a false self, to discharge the role of abdication and martyrdom. Images and words are the means for his own understanding of his part; they give it life for him, and for us. When he deals with images and words, he is far more effective than when he is trying to settle the dispute between Mowbray and Bolingbroke. It is in images and words that his greatness becomes visible. The part only exists as the words and images are found for it.

His greatness becomes visible on the stage—because he is

a stage figure, an actor demonstrating the truth of acting: he is a stage figure transferred into history. He imports there a flock of stage values and poetic values, which conflict with the political values of the story. It would have been possible to show a Richard whose susceptibility to self-dramatization ruined his political power. Shakespeare has done that to some extent, but he has done it with equivocation. For our delight in the words and images is not awakened to reinforce our sense of weakness of his character, in conflict with the "real" forces of the political world. Instead, the delight carries us toward an affirmation of the truth of dramatic poetry rather than the weakness of Richard's character or the strength of the political forces against him. Even at the last, this is the world which King Richard makes for himself in his cell. It is the world of the actor and the playwright. With the evocative eloquence and mystery of this world, a rival interpretation of the facts of the chronicle's story is held in waiting, and now it nudges, now it compels us to listen to it.

❧ 3 ❧

The Henriad:
Competitive Worlds

Does it make any further difference that the mystery of the actor's relation to this role is connected with the mystery of the divine and human king—as the king saw it—in the first of the plays of this *Richard II–Henry V* series? I think it does. For it is also the entering wedge of theatricality into the story where theater and reality keep approaching one another, and indeed substituting for one another. Richard II is a dramatic poet and actor deliberately tracing for us a road between the part he is acting and the form of truth which his acting creates before us. In the two parts of *Henry IV* the shape of the events, the plot, only superficially recalls the older linear progression of the history play. Instead, both the characters and the action are resolved into parallel and contrasting blocks which imitate one another, burlesque one another, or amplify the meaning one of the other, leaving no solid substance out of which the plot can operate with a single simple meaning.

James Winny, in *The Player King*,[1] has discussed the way in which Falstaff's Gadshill expedition and its outcome duplicate in comedy the relation between Henry IV (ex-Bolingbroke) and his nobles. The theft of the loot by Falstaff and the robbery of the thieves by Prince Hal and Poins are the comic version of Bolingbroke's acquisition of the crown and his subsequent quarrel with the Percies. Prince Hal imitates Hotspur, Hal and Falstaff between them imitate Hal and his father, then interchange roles. The two parts of *Henry V* (which as Dover Wilson points out are one play)[2] haunt us with the sense of imitation—as though no action could be noble or dignified without having a twin brother which is comic and absurd. Characters are paired in situation (the two princes, Hal and Percy, are again contrasted in King Henry's mind with himself and the dead Richard II, as they aspired to distinction and popularity), and again Falstaff and Percy are curiously interrelated, the one all fire and lyrical fervor, the other all comic cowardice and humor, and the worse one "kills" (symbolically at least) the better. This is a Shakespearean history of England which is itself turning into theater.

The early printed form of the play reads:[3] "The history of King Henry IV, with the battle of Shrewsbury between the king and Lord Henry Percy, surnamed Henry Hotspur of the north, with the humourous conceits of Sir John Falstaff." This certainly identifies three elements in the play: the history of the reign; the struggle with Hotspur, of which the battle of Shrewsbury is the climax; and Falstaff. It is very suggestive that one is being asked to see the reign of Henry IV under two added aspects of it, one high and one low. Is there perhaps a hint of a high and low contestant opposing the new establishment of Henry IV? This is what seems to be implied here. For as Percy menaces the king's crown,

Percy and Falstaff both, in different ways,[4] menace the future of that crown in the person of the Prince of Wales.

Hotspur is a kind of impersonator: that is, an actor who visibly uses his own personality as a sort of identifiable stage prop to express something else bigger and beyond it. Like Richard, he plays himself, but this is not a self which revels in its versatility. Apparently the actor who rendered the part used his personal defeats—some sort of stammer and some sort of limp—to make him unforgettably and singularly himself before our eyes. Lady Percy in *Henry IV, Part II* describes thus her dead husband:

> He was indeed the glass
> Wherein the noble youth did dress themselves.
> He had no legs that practised not his gait,
> And speaking thick (which nature made his blemish)
> Became the accents of the valiant.
>
> *(2H4* II.3.21)

His role is that of the poetic antipoet—so intensely set against literature and poetry in his passion for life and soldiership that his physical and mental being are the proof of the meaning of what he denounces.[5] The part has a luminosity of its own. In the battle scene, during which he rejected the king's demands for his prisoners, we can see just what a comic poet he is!

> My liege, I did deny no prisoners;
> But I remember, when the fight was done,
> When I was dry with rage and extreme toil,
> Breathless and faint, leaning upon my sword,
> Came there a certain lord, neat and trimly dress'd,
> Fresh as a bridegroom, and his chin new reap'd

> Show'd like a stubble land at harvest home.
> He was perfumed like a milliner,
> And 'twixt his finger and his thumb he held
> A pouncet-box, which ever and anon
> He gave his nose and took't away again . . .
> . . . and still he smil'd and talk'd;
> And as the soldiers bore dead bodies by,
> He call'd them untaught knaves, unmannerly,
> To bring a slovenly unhandsome corpse
> Betwixt the wind and his nobility—
> With many holiday and lady terms
> He questioned me; among the rest demanded
> My prisoners in your Majesty's behalf.
>
> (*1H4* I.3.29)

One can see how the ungainly limp and the stutter in mimicking the neat and trimly dressed lord brings out the very quality of derisiveness desired. Hotspur is a small man impersonating, and successfully so, for the benefit of our gallery, an impossible self seven feet tall.

In quite another mood is the intensity and excitement of the well-known passage:

> By Heaven, methinks it were an easy leap,
> To pluck bright honour from the pale-faced moon,
> Or dive into the bottom of the deep,
> Where fadom-line could never touch the ground,
> And pluck up drowned honour by the locks,
> So he that doth redeem her thence might wear
> Without corrival all her dignities.
>
> (*1H4* I.3.201)

This is stage poetry; it captures a truth expressible only on the stage with an actor's voice and gesture. But it also be-

longs to the particularity of this actor Hotspur. Only Hotspur will make entirely effective, with his clumsiness and explicit rejection of the conventional language of poetry, the
power of "And dive into the bottom of the deep / Where
fadom-line could never touch the ground." This moves the
individuality of the speaker and his emotion to a new area.
This area is more interesting, freer, and more real than the
actions and the motives of the main plot. The spell is on
us, almost directly, through the images of Hotspur's speech
which intervene vaguely between the character in the story
and ourselves. The scene with Hotspur's deliberate under-
playing of his affection for his wife, the teasing dialogue so
expressive of that affection, the other kind of teasing humor
in Hotspur's dealings with Glendower, extends the man in
his reality—as humorous observer, as lover, as whimsical
tetchy colleague. It hardly belongs to the story in any simple
sense. It creates a dimension of life before us which contrasts
powerfully with the texture of the main action—and not to
the advantage of the latter. The casual, almost incidental
glimpses of Percy's character, presumably reinforced by an
actor's playing with the individuality of his voice and movement, create a super-reality which dwarfs the other. We lose
feeling both for glory and humility when we resume the
watching of the tactics of the wild young man who eventually makes good.

The two *Henry IV* plays live from the tension between the
court of Henry IV and the two discordant elements, that re-
volving around Percy and that around Falstaff. The prince is
the link between the two. But the same tension also exists
between the moral positions of the story and the strength of
the imaginative values of the language both of Percy and Falstaff. The exuberance of the poetry and character of Hotspur
and the exuberance of the prose and the personality of Falstaff swamp our "proper" feelings for what is supposed to be

superior to them in the play. They work against the meaning of political success.

What is supposed to menace the development of Prince Hal into the future conqueror of France is a martial threat from the Percies and a threat from the evil communications of Falstaff and his friends. The Percies' rebellion is indeed the rivalry of a more princely prince in the person of Harry Hotspur ("Nor can one England brook a double reign / Of Harry Percy and the Prince of Wales" [*1H4* V.4.66). Falstaff is shown as the center of the fun and horseplay which are in their anarchic fashion the antithesis of the dignity of the English crown the prince is to inherit. Of course, we as an audience are prepared for the final defeat of the Percies. We are also prepared for the final rejection of Falstaff and the end of Hal's crop of wild oats.

But what happens to us as we read or see is something different from what we are prepared for and what is "proper." What menaces the future of England, in the challenge of the "proper" Prince Hal, is the challenge to our imagination made by Percy's character and poetry and the inspired and overwhelming comic power of Falstaff expressed by the prose in which it is clothed. We are totally overwhelmed by the sense of barriers removed, in passion and understanding, by the words of both. The achievement of Henry IV, that now blameless and effective sovereign, only troubled by his son's disreputability, becomes the correct varnished surface of the court poetry, acting as a backdrop for the struggle for Hal's soul, which is presented in the incomparable dialogues between Falstaff and the Prince. Even the death of Percy and the rejection of Falstaff touch us less than the stretching of our imagination which both figures inspire in us, by the styles associated with them. What one gains finally from the poetry is not exactly, or at least not only, a sharper definition of the characters, but the vision of some country where the passionate truth exceeds the range of any particular character, and where the attention is riveted by images that grow or diminish with slender or indeterminate relation to their speakers.

Not only Hal but the whole structure of the historical fabric of events and the values traditionally assigned to them are in danger. For the theater's resources are being made to bear testimony against the history that it is imitating. Here is Hal's mimed characterization of the very Hotspur whose speech on honor has made such a mark on us. "I am not yet of Percy's mind, the Hotspur of the north, he that kills me some six or seven dozen of Scots at a breakfast, washes his hands, and says to his wife 'Fie upon this quiet life! I want work.'" "Oh my sweet Harry," says she, "How many hast thou kill'd today?" "Give my roan horse a drench," says he, and answers "some fourteen," an hour later; "a trifle, a trifle I prithee call up Falstaff. I'll play Percy and the damn'd brawn shall play Dame Mortimer his wife . . ." (1H4 II.4.112). The burlesquing of the serious elements of the story reaches its high point in the charade which Hal contrives between himself and Falstaff, representing the king his father and himself—and then they interchange the parts (1H4 II.4.442). The play we are watching is using all the actor's talents of imitation, for tragedy and comedy, to render a world which is turning into theater itself. There is a continual expansion of mood, refusal to render an event or a character univocally; the nature of the imitation for elevation or amusement is becoming the criterion of all real difference in the way we see the story. Therefore it becomes harder to believe in a story, as an imitation of reality, which can accommodate the scope of all the different styles as a dimension of life.

The play also at least once explores with brutal shock the

values of an independent theatricality—that is, the direct theatricality of the improvising clown rather than the actor and
the mime. We have grown to be very fond of Hotspur. His
death on the battlefield, at the hands of the Prince of Wales,
is the somber, noble conclusion to the rivalry between the
two princely princes. This is exactly how Hal expresses it in
his valedictory address to the body.

> This earth that bears thee dead
> Bears not alive so stout a gentleman.
> If thou wert sensible of courtesy
> I should not make so dear a show of zeal:
> But let my favors hide thy mangled face,
> And even in thy behalf I'll thank myself
> For doing these fair rites of tenderness
> Adieu and take thy praise with thee to Heaven!
> Thy ignomy sleep with thee in the grave
> But not remember'd in thy epitaph.
>
> *(1H4* V.4.92)

Whereupon the seemingly dead Falstaff rises, stabs the body
of Percy and lugs it off, to be the proof of his nonexistent
valor and the first stepping stone to his future preferment.
Thus the whole incident of Percy's death becomes altered.
Whatever we may prefer, we cannot continue our sense of
its unequivocal significance. It has been turned over to the
clown and in his version represents the superiority of cowardice's good sense over valor's sense of glory, of laughter
over tears, of cunning hypocrisy over the single-minded devotion to "higher" values. The roaring comic power of Falstaff here is employed to destroy the fabric of the history, in
its obvious and immediate sense; Falstaff uses Hotspur's body
as a stage prop with which to take us quite away from the

solidity of illusion with which the playwright has been con-
fronting us. In the place of this solidity has come another
illusion, where the range of sorrow and pleasure has been
extended toward one another and both made dependent on
the performance of a special interpreter. We do not believe in
the reality of Falstaff's appropriation of Percy's body in the
same way that we have just been led to believe in Percy's
death. But we are suddenly switched to a mood where both
the story and our serious reception of it is subjected to a
searchlight whose beams throw it into a new relief. The
clowning of Falstaff is contrived, as the rendering of Percy's
death is not. But the contrivance hints at the fundamental
ambiguity of all the tragic or comic moods which the story
would assert to be singular. We know Hotspur and Kate very
well indeed—and care for them. There is something important about the theatrical annihilation of (or, at least, assault
on) this sympathy.

The two characters, Hotspur and Falstaff, are related not
only in their political and social challenges to Prince Hal's
future; they repeat the high and the low challenge, to politics,
and statecraft, in feeling and passion and laughter and irresponsibility. The effect is finally to lock politics and political
history into an area where certain of our responses never en-
ter at all. The emotions which belong with the part where
we are responsive go with the extravagance of speech of
Percy and Falstaff in its appeal to the imagination. They
themselves also create a standard of meaningfulness from
which the main events recoil and pale.

In his abdication Richard is an actor giving theatrical substance to the divinity of the king; but Shakespeare's art, in
catching this reality, has its corollary in Falstaff's mocking
imitation of the interview of king and prince, and then in the
prince's mimed version of the same scene, and again in the

prince's version of the conversation of Hotspur and his wife. The tragic emotion of Richard is an actor's emotion and it has an actor's truth. Hotspur's extravagant nobility comes to us by means of the impersonator's art where the actor uses himself—his peculiar bodily attitude and voice—like an instrument to reveal a special meaning. The bitterness of Hotspur's death fades into laughter to see his stabbed body become the comic means of Falstaff's elevation, because, then, Falstaff has become the clown playing directly to us rather than to the other actors. The story starts with a king who understands his kingship as an actor understands the reality of his performance, at the supreme moment of his playing. It ends with a competition between the art of the theater and the meaning of "real" events in history.

I have hitherto considered Hotspur and Falstaff as they challenge the treatment of the history theme and as they dent the surface of theatrical representation. Let us now look at the play through Hal's eyes, which means reacting to his theatrical strategems.

In the two parts of *Henry IV,* Shakespeare has deliberately reduced the role of King Henry IV himself. Dover Wilson has shown how he has played havoc with the time scheme to compress the reign.[6] Shakespeare has also compressed the character of the king until what we have of it turns only on a hinge of unhappiness and dissatisfaction. The monarchy he has seized is poisoned for him by his guilt toward Richard; his immediate present is threatened by his doubts of his ability to handle the revolt; his hopes of the future are shaky because of the conduct of the Prince of Wales. This is a study of a transitional reign. The solution is all dependent on Hal, and as a result Hal dominates formally both parts of the play. It seems to be due to his unexpected bravery, as Dover Wilson shows, that Henry's forces beat the Percies.[7] It is due to the Prince's transformation of his private life that Henry's worst cares for the future of his kingdom are relieved on his deathbed. His burden of guilt for Richard, deposed and killed, he bequeaths to Hal, and we find in the night before Agincourt that Henry V has assumed his father's obligation. If he feels freer in handling this than his father, that is reasonable enough. But the guilt, objectively, is still there, and forges a connection backward in composition but forward in dramatic time to Henry VI's ruminations on the validity of his title to the crown. Shakespeare's play, *Henry V,* whether or not based on *The Famous Victories of Henry V,* is a kind of epilogue. When the victory for Prince Hal's character is won, and the rebellion of the Percies suppressed, *Henry V* comes into its own.

The framework of *Henry IV* is one where the Prince is learning to be a successful king but is learning on his own terms. He is stage-managing the show. He will utilize Falstaff and his friends as a backdrop against which his final emergence as a great prince will be the more glorious. His rival, Hotspur, will be only his factor, one who earns glory which, when its owner is defeated, will belong to Hal the conqueror (*1H4* III.2.147). What gives the play life in spite of its cold-blooded setting is Hal's temptation on the way.

Hal is not disguised, and he exercises no manipulative function comparable to that of the Duke of Vienna in *Measure for Measure.* He does not do anything special to the Falstaff-Poins contingent. He simply makes one of them. He implies that he likes them and is willing, or nearly willing, to do anything that they do. His remark over the presumably dead Falstaff, "I could have better spared a better man" (*2H4* V.4.104), even indicates a certain genuineness in the affection for Falstaff, and indeed there is an undercurrent of real feeling in nearly all the scenes between the Prince and Falstaff. None of this undermines the toughness of the relation on both sides. Hal is a part of the Falstaff company for reasons of his own (which Warwick may or may not have hit off [*2H4* IV.4.67]); Falstaff and Poins and the lesser fry are avowedly glad of the Prince's company as valuable insurance against trouble in the present and as a hope of indefinite license in the future.

Of the two sides of this association there is no doubt about the "why" as far as the rogues go. What about the Prince? Do we in fact know why Hal makes friends with Falstaff and Poins and courts their society? The following soliloquy is the most explicit piece of evidence in the play on what the Prince means to do by his deception of his "friends."

> I know you all and will awhile uphold
> The unyok'd humour of your idleness.
> Yet herein I will imitate the sun,
> Who doth permit the base contagious clouds
> To smother up his beauty from the world,
> That when he please again to be himself,
> Being wanted, he may be more wond'red at,
> By breaking through the foul and ugly mists
> Of vapours that did seem to strangle him . . .
> So when this loose behaviour I throw off
> And pay the debt I never promised,
> By how much better than my word I am,
> By so much shall I falsify men's hopes . . .
>
> (*1H4* I.2.196)

The disguise, then, is designed to present in its most brilliant colors his true personality, when it finally emerges. He is in fact playing a role, building it to a conscious denouement

which will come only after his father's death. He is the stuff
of heroes and the future king in the fight at Shrewsbury; but
he is shown as falling back into his "disguise" of the young
debauchee who is knocking about low taverns in London
when his father is dying. The moment for his final entrance
is not yet. This is still to be prefaced with some scenes which
will make everyone believe that the heroic bits were only
flashes in the pan, and that the real prince is the no-good his
father and everyone else so long have thought him.

It seems likely enough that Shakespeare is anxious not to
throw any real mud on the royal hero Henry V at a time
when these patriotic plays were particularly in vogue. It is
notable, for instance, that even when Hal joins in the Gadshill robbery the booty taken is restored by his royal orders.
In other scenes Hal is merely the onlooker at Falstaff's in-
volvement—as in the Doll Tearsheet episodes. In the one
where Hal bears a part—the interlude with the drawer Fran-
cis—what the Prince does is entirely innocent, except insofar
as his acts derogate from the royal dignity.

The general charge against the Prince would seem to lie
entirely in the matter of his association with companions of
lower class; the general fear for the future lies in the assumption that these same companions will have their way with
him when he becomes king. Now we, from the vantage
point that his soliloquy allows us, see no evidence that any of
his associates can get him to do anything they want. But
there's no mistaking that Hal enters into the mood of a series
of tableaux, and that this mood, which is invariably irrespon-
sible, mocking at morality and the seriousness of the court
and its designs, challenges indeed the weight of the political
fabric of the story that is being told us. This mood in Prince
Hal is really a conscious escape from the part of a prince. In
dealing with the Bohemians of Eastcheap the Prince is releas-

ing himself into a region of unqualified, unpolitical humanity. He knows that this is what he is doing—and it is here that the risk really lies. For this temptation to irresponsibility is hardly adequately covered by his original pious strategy. He, in his *potential* self, knows the temptation of acting in its contest with royalty. The temptation is not to be himself but a number of other selves not consistent with the role of king-ruler.

In the soliloquy I have quoted the emphasis is heavily on the determining part played by the Prince. "I will awhile uphold / The unyok'd humour of your idleness." This presumably means that he will tolerate the characteristic vice of Falstaff and his circle—that they do nothing useful or functional in the state and please themselves in the "Unyok'd-ness." But when the suitable dramatic moment has come, when the revelation of his true character will have the maximum effect on his future subjects, when indeed by being displayed at that moment it will achieve results impossible for a more steadily proper prince—then Hal will show himself like the sun escaping from "the base contagious clouds." The plan is almost inhumanly designed and intentionally constructed. There is no hint of some inner uncertainty or weakness of intention, such as apparently Dr. Johnson found when he said that the Prince was subject to vices from which he perhaps "momentarily could not free himself."

The Earl of Warwick in his conversation with King Henry IV supports the Prince's avowed theory of his disguise as follows.

> My gracious Lord, you look beyond him quite.
> The Prince but studies his companions,
> Like a strange tongue, wherein to gain the language
> 'Tis needful that the most immodest word

Be look'd upon and learnt—which once attain'd,
Your Highness knows, comes to no further use,
But to be known and hated. So, like gross terms,
The Prince will in the perfectness of time
Cast off his followers, and their memory
Shall as a pattern or a measure live
By which his Grace must mete the lives of others
Turning past evils to advantages.

(2H4 IV.4.67)

What is implied here is the total separation, in feeling and understanding, between subject and king. The king must, in fact, learn like a strange tongue the "pattern" of the lives of those he rules. We may assume that later Henry V does indeed put his training to advantage. Presumably his relations to the ordinary soldiers in the French campaign are the outcome of his contact with waiters, highwaymen, etc. It is remarkable throughout this chronicle how much is made of the necessary popular contact between king and commoner. Whether this is really a shadow of Plantagenet days or a much more contemporary reflection of the late Tudors one can only guess.

Falstaff and Poins occupy an extreme position in this language. They are the obscenities, the ostentatious flouting of the decencies. The obscenities live in the borderline country where their use represents an escape, temporary and more or less controlled, from the submerged and often more significant decencies. What gives life and meaning to Prince Hal's otherwise cold-blooded stratagem to teach himself to be a prince (by observing even the most vulgar of his fellow countrymen) is that he *is* tempted by the human obscenity Falstaff; although he never ceases to be the Prince that will one day be king, there are moments when he most willingly abandons the stiffness of the formalized posture and opinions of the prince for the assumption of irresponsibility, moral and social. This is what he says himself at the moment when he associates with the waiter: "I am now of all humours that have show'd themselves humours since the old days of good-man Adam to the pupil age of this present twelve a'clock at midnight" (*1H4* II.4.91). And it is interesting that directly afterwards, his first comment on the wretched waiter is "that ever this fellow should have fewer *words* than a parrot, and yet the son of a woman!" He then goes on to deride the ostentatious shortness of speech of Percy, which he proposes to parody with Falstaff's help, as we saw earlier. For the purposes of the play Hal does immerse himself in Eastcheap, but not very much in whorings, drunkenness, or more serious escapades. The real escape lies in the indulgence in a limitless vocabulary of abuse, amusement, description, which stems from Falstaff and where Hal, in his unprincely pose, bears his very fair share.

Falstaff is not an ordinary sort of actor who takes a role and interprets it. He is rather the spirit of the theater itself in one of its aspects—that of the clown. The clown creates in visible form before us—very visible form indeed in the bulk of Falstaff—the mood of our fantasy, especially the fantasy which is rebellious, irregular, lecherous, cowardly, disloyal. In this play there is a weighting of sympathy and enjoyment between the pointless and inconsequential buffoonery—and the consequential politics. It is no good saying (with Dover Wilson) that the Elizabethan audience would of course feel as respectable people should between the two, but would all the same enjoy Falstaff.[8] That is in a sense perfectly true—as far as the outline of the story goes. But something happens to us when our sense of enjoyment is so acutely tickled as it is by Falstaff's words and Falstaff's massiveness and Falstaff's helplessness, finally.

Now Hal is a temporary visitor in this stage world; true, he is even briefly an accomplice in it, in the abuse and the laughing melancholy that shape the scenes between himself and Falstaff. But he is only a very temporary visitor or accomplice. When he sees what he takes to be the dead Falstaff at Shrewsbury, he says, "O I should have had a heavy miss of thee / If I were much in love with vanity" (*1H4* V.4.105). He is certainly not as much in love with vanity as we the audience are—or as I am sure the Elizabethan audience was— for he represented the future king of England.

What is gradually established about Falstaff is that the old man has no function in real life except to be a buffoon. He imagines that what he hears from Shallow will give him raw material for amusing the Prince for months—without realizing that the Prince's holidays are over (*2H4* V.1.85). What Shakespeare has done is to give us the world of buffoonery where nothing serious can live, and everything funny has a preternatural life, and gives it to us as the desirable world. The Prince remains squarely in the middle. The laughter and exuberance of Falstaff is in the play *Henry IV* a rebel emotion. It will allow no quarter to dignity, nor the assumptions of morality, nor the necessity of duty. This constitutes a root-and-branch attack on tragedy and the meaning of political history. "My lord, I was born about three of the clock in the afternoon, with a white head and something of a round belly. For my voice, I have lost it with hallooing and singing of anthems. To approve my youth further, I will not. The truth is, I am only old in judgement and understanding" (*2H4* I.2.187); and "banish not him thy Harry's company, banish plump Jack, and banish all the world!" (*1H4* II.4.479).

There remains to make some sense of one's own jumbled and ambiguous impressions of the play *Henry V.* This is, of course, the final stage of the success story of the unpromising prince who made good. It should be the clincher to the underlying general theme—the emergence of the proper king, national hero, conqueror of France, secure on his throne, efficient in his government, his legitimacy, if not completely satisfactory as he himself still feels in the soliloquy the night before Agincourt, at least well established practically, and its defects compensated for by the prayers of the poor and the pious (*H5* IV.1.297)—as King Henry explains to us.

It would all be alright, or mostly alright, if it were not for the way in which the loss of Falstaff is obtruded on our attention, both in his deathbed scene, in the casual comments on the relations of the king and himself, and in the much poorer substitutes which Shakespeare has found for the dramatic value which is the fat man's, in contrast with the political world.

Falstaff was the almost-clown, rather than actor, with a direct approach to his audience. When he is telling of how Hal had put a spell on him, or vows that he will not "be damned for e'er a king's son in Christendom," of course we are the listeners to whom he is speaking. He is our particular delight, our safety valve for all our antipolitical and antinoble sentiments in this great court and war panorama. We know that the Falstaff mood and temper, which we enjoy, must be enjoyed surreptitiously and harmonized with the full sense of responsibility. And Shakespeare deliberately baits the promise of the new play with prospects of Falstaff in France (*2H4* Epilogue). No doubt Kemp's disappearance had a great deal to do with Shakespeare's inability to keep his word. But I doubt if it has everything to do with it.

Even if Falstaff had to be written off because that actor and that role had become so identified as to be inseparable, this does not account for the jarring of our susceptibilities by the depth of the Hostess' simple, "He'll yield the crow a pudding

one of these days. The King has kill'd his heart" (*H5* II.1.90).
We see the accuracy of Nym's idiotically comic notice of Falstaff and Henry, "The King hath run bad humours on the
knight, that's the even of it. The King is a good king, but it
must be as it may; he passes some humours and careers" (*H5*
II.1.121). Even when the first moments of the play are over,
and we could forget Falstaff, we are brought back again to
him by Fluellen's parody of Alexander, who killed his friend
Cleitus. Fluellen deliberately compares this with Henry's
turning away of Falstaff (*H5* IV.7.45). Shakespeare wants us
to realize what Falstaff's loss means.

There will be the conventional elements in the presentation
of Henry's character—the conventional heroics, and the conventional conscience of the king at Agincourt, and the conventional bravery and perspicacity with which he unmasks
the traitors at his court. But these things are made to go
along with the hypocrisy of Henry's interrogation of the
clergy about the Salic law—after the Archbishop has told us
of the impending threat of confiscation of Church property,
with the dreadful menace to the mayor of Harfleur, featuring
the rape and plunder of the town and the murder of children;
with the actual killing of the prisoners of war; with the pious
notice of the hanging of poor old red-nosed Bardolph. It is
probably wrong to say that *Henry V* is a study in irony.
There is hardly enough of it, and Shakespeare can leave us in
no doubt about his irony when he has a mind to, as we can
see in *Troilus and Cressida*. But it seems truer to say that, than
to accept, as Dover Wilson does,[9] the whole of the implied
comment in *Henry V* as a "proper" patriotic sentiment.[10]
This is a harsh play, for all that it is a national epic—the only
play that Shakespeare wrote in celebration of a *successful* war-
rior-politician.[11]

The comedy too has become conventionalized. Bardolph,

Nym, and Pistol are simply there to express amusingly a lighter side of things than the political and military. They do not deliberately parody the serious and weighty as Falstaff and his Gadshill robbery did. The three captains—the Welshman, the Scot, and the Irishman—are straights; the joke is on the accent and the temperaments, both entirely stock. And the conscience-tortured king and the disguised king who hears the dilemma of the simple subject and plays simple jokes with him in return—well, the play certainly brings together an odd assortment.

There is no doubt that the play *Henry V* is designed to show the successful and heroic King Henry against the failure (that is, political failure) Richard II. What values Shakespeare has assigned to the two is of course a very different matter, but these values live inside the stage reality of the two men. Henry V's success is straightforward and definite. He inherits his share of his father's guilt for the deposition of Richard—but he has taken care of that, insofar as can be, by paid-for prayers. He follows his father's advice for distracting his possibly rebellious nobles by a foreign campaign—and instead of the Crusade which Bolingbroke planned and never achieved, there is the glorious winning of France; the actual rebels in his kingdom are effortlessly discovered and punished by the king. His own former base associates are got rid of. All of this is conveyed by the right sort of poetry which Yeats characterized as "resounding rhetoric." This is ruling, this is politics, in its ordinary manifestations. But in Richard II (the other king), although at the very end of his reign, one is aware of another value. With every vice and weakness which destroy his kingship (seen as ruler), Richard still is God's servant, now appointed to the task for formal self-annihilation. The gift of the actor is to become aware of one of his latent selves, in its connection with the part dictated to him. He does so using all he has learned about voices, gesture, and movement. The process is mysterious, since the new self only comes into existence as he plays him. Richard recognizes some intermediate being, not himself and not quite another, who performs God's will in destroying himself-that-was-king, in the ceremony of abdication. He invents a ritual for his renunciation. As we watch King Richard creating a new Martyr Richard, we see a new meaning to person and role in the context of reality. A new kingship is created before our eyes.

4

English and Roman History: A Contrast

In the "true" history plays, both English and to some extent Roman, the great historical events—especially the victories and defeats with their political consequences—overlap the probabilities established in our minds by the action and characters of the people involved as we follow them through the play. Overlap and in the end largely nullify them. In the English historical plays there is an outer area and an inner. The inner is vividly illuminated. It offers us characters, beliefs, ideals; all sorts of potentialities, likelihoods, hopes and fears. The outer area is murky and solid. This is where "history" is, the great events which were presumably decisive. They happened—and therefore they permanently negate all the other potentialities of character and opportunity of which we have become aware. Here is the overwhelming catastrophe of Richard II, when because of a single day's delay and the superstition of the Welsh commander all his military chances are at an end. No convincing dramatic link is made in the play between the ruin and the hesitations, weaknesses, ill-doing, which we know from the king's conduct at the beginning of the story. They are there as evidence against him, yes. We feel that a king like that will not long survive as king. But it is the almost accidental factors of timing which prove decisive. To some degree history within the play is a kind of pageant, without the purposeful compression of action into a satisfying imaginative coherence. The pageant is a suitable rendering of history because there is a conflict between history and drama and this must be rendered. The imagination cannot entirely master the facts—or they will not constitute history. Instead, it is led to contemplate with awe the final act in the story—the reversal and overthrow of greatness—the Wheel of Fortune. The pageant, the Wheel of Fortune aspect, lives in disconnectedness from the preparation of dramatic likelihood.

What later becomes the preparation of dramatic likelihoods, which are neither chronicles nor histories, is already being taken over in *Richard II* by the immense increase in depth and complexity which Shakespeare is giving one part of the historical theme. He still retains nearly the whole structure of the story, even if it does not concern his emphasis. Bolingbroke wins, because he won in history. But the play is concerned with far more than that. It covers what happened inside Richard's mind when he first finds himself defeated, and then later as captive awaiting death. The formal outline is filled in, but our vital perceptions and sympathy recognize it as something factual and outside the range of dramatic concern. The alienation from history of the lively, rich, and humanly explanatory parts of the story is greatest in *Henry IV, Part I* and *II,* where Falstaff and his relation to Hal have stolen the dramatic meaning of the piece; but here the parody of the higher by the lower part certainly suggests a commentary and common criterion. This play (treating Parts I and II as one in conjunction) is unique in that while it belongs to the type of the older chronicle plays, it has a most original frame of reference embracing its parts.

In the classical plays the linear arbitrariness of the older pageant of events is almost at an end. The pursuit of power is a much more convincing key to all the action and its consequences than in *Richard II* or even the Henriad, for now this appetite is being studied in depth and there are only a few fragments of undramatized history. Power itself in *Julius Caesar* is mysterious in its concentration, diffusion, and again concentration in other despotic bands.

> O Julius Caesar, thou are mighty yet!
> Thy spirit walks abroad, and turns our swords
> In our own proper entrails.
>
> (*JC* V.3.92)

The weight of this play, in harmony with the story behind it, is purely political. It is the mysterious nature of power, as sought for and exercised, that holds the center of the scene: how it corrupts and distorts the ethics of private life and the idealism of those who seek it; how it suggests virtues and vices of quite a different order from those of the private person altogether. The course set by the rivals in the struggles for power is the pattern of destiny for most of mankind, leaders and victims alike. This play stresses mostly what happens to the leaders—though of course one is aware, in the background, of the soldiers sacrificed in the battle and the towns plundered and the persons murdered by proscriptions. For the leaders, then, the pattern becomes a baleful fate, impersonal as the gods in Sophocles. Its distinguishing mark is that

the more complex and rich the character that engages in political life—in this play the pursuit of power rather than the
day-to-day exercise of it—the more certain it is that such a
man will not be the eventual winner.

> There is a tide in the affairs of men
> which taken at the flood, leads on to fortune;
> omitted, all the voyage of their life
> is bound in shallows and in miseries.
>
> (*JC* IV.3.217)

Those who navigate most successfully the moment of the
flood are neither Brutus nor even Antony, but that colorless
and effortless chooser of the correct course, Octavian, the
later Augustus. Though Antony has effectually put him in
the possession of his opportunity, it is not Antony but Octavian who takes upon himself the role of protagonist against
the "liberators."

> Look,
> I draw a sword against conspirators;
> When think you that the sword goes up again?
> Never till Caesar's three and thirty wounds
> Be well aveng'd, or till another Caesar
> Have added slaughter to the sword of Traitors.
>
> (*JC* V.1.51)

Of course, politics are politics as much in the chronicle
plays as in the Roman. In both, men's ambition, greed, and
envy are the inner force of political change, as much in *Richard II* as in *Julius Caesar*. But the apparatus of politics is different and leads to a bleaker effect in the Roman plays. In the
chronicle plays the king is the head of what is regarded as a

divinely appointed order: those who deal with him do not do so simply, as with an autocrat like Caesar. Even the winning politician like Bolingbroke, when he becomes Henry IV, does not shake off the guilt of sacrilege that he incurred when he destroyed his predecessor on the throne. Neither Antony nor Octavian has any such conscientious scruples to contend with in the removal of rivals in their ambition. Cassius and Brutus speak of the murder of Casear as an act of universal significance. The dramatic repetition, which they look forward to, suggests its final truth. One is at first inclined to see the Roman tyrannicide as the celebration of a continuing meaning.

> *Cas.* Stoop then, and wash. How many ages hence
> Shall this our lofty scene be acted o'er,
> In states unborn and accents yet unknown!
>
> *Bru.* How many times shall Caesar bleed in sport,
> That now on Pompey's basis lies along
> No worthier than the dust!
>
> *Cas.* So oft as that shall be,
> So often shall the knot of us be call'd
> The men that gave their country liberty.
> (*JC* III.1.111)

But as one gets on with the play there is a curious ambivalence in the contrast between this theatrically heralded act and the reality of its consequences. Brutus *has* validated the murder by the symbolic dipping of the hands in blood: this *is* the first of a series of echoing mimetic performances. But he and his associates have not perceived the true meaning of the performance they are giving. It is surely ironical that the murderers see themselves as "the men who gave their country liberty" when this very play sees the end of the liberty they gave and when this failure of aim is certainly indicated as the typical outcome. Their reflection on the repetition of the act as *play* ("How many times shall Caesar bleed *in sport*") as opposed to the reality of the assassination has the odd quality of calling in question the very meaning which its institutors felt it asserted. Here, say Brutus and Cassius, is how liberty was rescued, and this is how future ages will act it out. We find ourselves adding: how like theater that is, and how unlike the harsh, unique aspect of truth which will overtake this act.

The Roman plays have one feature of politics missing in the chronicles. Their leading statesmen are, partially at least, obsessed by the notion of personal models. Brutus lives in the shadow of his great ancestor who drove out Tarquin; Coriolanus in the shadow of the ideals of the perfect aristocrat, perfect soldier, perfect son, which he has received from his mother. Antony lives until his last moment by the ideal behind the words "but please your thoughts / in feeding them with those my former fortunes / wherein I liv'd, the greatest prince o' th' world, / the noblest; and do now not basely die, / not cowardly put off my helmet to / my countryman—a Roman by a Roman / valiantly vanquish'd (*Ant.* IV.15.54).

These models belong to a moral climate more rarified than that of the catch-as-catch-can game of practical politics. Indeed there is a constant tension between the ordinary demands of politics and this attitude of the leaders, based on something different. The greater the tension, the greater the political failure. The Roman models involve a kind of role-playing; but the roles are sharply prescriptive: they are indeed charts of moral conduct, and as such override the flexible mental engineering called for in each political situation. But noticeably they do not make for the mysterious but vague identification which united Richard the fallen king with the suffering Christ, as a figure of sacred myth.

The failure of the Roman leader, in these plays, is often because of the conflict between his broadly prescriptive role and the definition of the actual political situation. Brutus acquits Caesar, in his own mind, of the acts of a tyrant. He must be killed because of his position as virtual dictator and his potential kingship. So far, the model of Brutus the Elder (our Brutus's ancestor) with relation to the Tarquin carries our Brutus into the conspiracy and the murder. But Brutus's distinction between Caesar's personal innocence and functional guilt is a prelude to his big mistake in not killing Antony. Antony is as innocent and guilty as Caesar. His death is as much a necessity for the preservation of the new order as Casear's was for the destruction of the former one. But here Brutus has no longer his model to guide him, or rather he has too much model to guide him. It was a model of a certain sort of intensely moral man, and all the more because it is directed to the sacrifice of any personal feelings. We must not forget the story of the elder Brutus's readiness to send his sons to death.

In the light of this model, Brutus is very ready to sacrifice his own sentiments of affection, gratitude, and loyalty to Caesar in the name of principle. But it is really the personal sacrifice, as a sign of genuine inspiration, that is leading him on. This becomes quite clear in Brutus's very tepid assessment of what real harm Caesar has done and the emphasis on his own sacrifice in killing his friend. Brutus felt no special friendship but also no repugnance for Antony, nothing in fact but a mild contempt. He has nothing therefore to entice him to act in this like Brutus the Elder, nothing to sacrifice. The killing of Antony is only a dirty matter of practical politics, and Brutus's own uninfluenced sentiments of fairness and justice prevail to spare him. It is, however, typical of him that his last word on the matter is an altogether incorrect estimate of popular feeling: "Our course will seem too bloody, Caius Cassius, / to cut the head off and then hack the limbs." But the bloodiness of the proscription has in the play no apparent effect on public opinion.

These hero roles in the Roman plays inflict on their enactors a kind of dislocated drama. They are committed to failure but can hardly attain to the aesthetic satisfaction of tragedy, and this is, in a way, because the Roman models do not allow of enough free space for the generation of personal elements in the acting. Richard's identification with the betrayed and suffering Christ is an intensely personal thing; yet no action is prescribed him—only a union of position and emotion. Consequently his staging of the abdication is an autonomous free creation which fulfilled his new imaginative concept of himself within the framework of the Passion. But Brutus and Coriolanus are allotted almost narrowly prescribed courses of action in order to demonstrate the truth of what they stand for. These prove their undoing in politics. Coriolanus of course fails to execute the part his mother assumes is so easy. Brutus mismanages the speech in the Forum, because he is *trying* to be rational and open while rhetorical and is baffled by the melodramatic claptrap of Antony which gets the audience. The same sort of "Roman foolishness" in Antony in the later *Antony and Cleopatra* is brutally answered by Octavius in response to Antony's challenge to a dual: "Let the old ruffian know / I have many other ways to die" (*Ant.* IV.1.4.).

There is something very like derogatory realism in Shakespeare's presentation of the classical models of wisdom, bravery, political virtue, and, one might add, political life itself.

Could an autocrat be shown as vainer, littler, more irresolute than Caesar, contrasted with his "But I am constant as the northern star / of whose true-fix'd and resting quality / there is no fellow in the firmament" (*JC* III.1.60)? And Brutus? True, Brutus is the champion of freedom. But what an amount of uncomfortable humanization there is about the portrait! He has a very exalted sense of honor, but his friendship need not be depended on too much—see his treatment of Caesar and Cassius. Friendship is always running up against this sense of duty of his, and getting much the worse of it. He shows stoic endurance at the news of his wife's death, but we, unlike the unsuspecting Messala, know that he was aware of the fact before Messala tells him and admires him for his calm resignation. His views of suicide when expounded to Cassius first are impressive:

> I know now how,
> but I do find it cowardly and vile,
>
> (*JC* V.1.103)

but later he changes:

> Think not, thou noble Roman,
> That ever Brutus will go bound to Rome.
> He bears too great a mind
>
> (*JC* V.1.110)

—and finally he kills himself. None of these inconsistencies makes Brutus a bad man or vicious or a hypocrite. They merely make him human—but they significantly alter the heroic classical proportions of the freedom fighter.

In the English chronicle plays the top levels of political man—the king, the nobility, the fighting gentry—are at least superficially gilded with dignity, and their acts with an air of patriotism and importance. No such elevating atmosphere attends the politics of the classical world. It is a dog-eat-dog affair. Nothing like the proscription in *Julius Caesar* is to be found in the chronicles, for large-scale preventive butchery. It is worth remembering that it is a fact of Roman history and perhaps impressed Shakespeare as just such a horribly unique fact.

There is also no mistaking the note of pessimistic criticism of the internal dissension and instability of the Roman state. In the chronicle plays there is danger to a weak king from his nobles—see the case of *Richard II* or *Henry VI*. Even for the strong kings like Henry IV and V rebellion is always a possibility to be watched. But it is in *Julius Caesar* that Shakespeare shows us a state where there is no system at all for the orderly succession of one power holder by another. Brutus's (and Cassius's) dream of a collective authority of the Optimates is a dream and no more. The voice of the man in the crowd is prophetic when, as he expresses his enthusiasm for Brutus's denunciation of the fallen tyrant, he exclaims, "Let him (Brutus) be Caesar!" (*JC* III.2.51). This is a Rome where one Caesar can only be succeeded by another—as Octavian knows. Whether this has been brought to pass by Caesar himself, or whether the earlier Republican government was already a shaky combination of jealous oligarchs and dangerous military men, and sank, almost of its own weight, Shakespeare does not certainly indicate, and we should not read our version of Roman history into the background of this play. But at the least, the play is perfectly clear that there is going to be no restoration of collective responsibility in *Julius Caesar*—only a question whether the party of the conspirators or the party of the Triumvirs will succeed the dead dictator and, afterwards, which single autocrat will emerge.

Since one Caesar must succeed another and there is no formal acknowledgment of how the office must be continued, there will almost always be war—depending on the strength of the rival claimants to the effective nucleus of power. Compared with this, the Wars of the Roses are a particular and almost an accidental phenomenon.

Inside the Roman plays the background of politics is Hobbesian—the war of all against all. Part of what remains ambiguous is whether the play also affirms a positive value in the concentration of power, even in a dictator, and even in such a humanly insignificant dictator as Caesar is as the play opens. Granted he is no king—yet, at least, does he not, simply by existing, have some of the political merits of the royal authority? Is Brutus wrong, not only because he continually values the abstract and general over what is alive and personal, but because he destroys the only viable concentration of peaceful government of Rome, however precarious?

There is no missing, too, the adverse verdict on the Roman concept of freedom, as it lives in the play. The dynamic of politics lies with the plebeians and not only with their votes but with their power to murder, burn, and destroy at the urging of demagogues like Antony. It is true that Caesar shows a certain fear of public opinion among the Optimates, when Decius Brutus hints that if rebuffed or put off they may later decline to give the crown to Caesar. We must not forget that we start this play at a crucial moment, when Caesar is on the point of changing his complicated and vaguely indicated status for a single title expressing his power. To get the mechanics of the process arranged needs careful handling. In this respect the Optimates may have a certain temporary value. But the real trial balloon for sovereignty had gone up at the Lupercal when Antony offered Caesar the crown— undoubtedly at Caesar's orders. It is the crowd of honest, sweaty, nightcapped neighbors of the disgruntled Casca whose approval is sought, and on whom the whole thing finally depends. It is this same crowd that eventually overwhelms the conspirators and murders the innocent Cinna. It is those who know best how to control them—like Antony—those who then are able and cold-blooded enough to eliminate from the Optimates anyone able enough to challenge the leadership, who profit by the blind mindless substructure of all power in Rome.

In this play, as surely as there is no institution of monarch to safeguard the community against civil war, so neither is there protection of law for the security of property and liberty for the individual. Perhaps Shakespeare might have liked to be quoted in the words of Charles I uttered at his execution, fifty years after *Richard II,* at the end of the Great Rebellion, "As for the people, truly I desire their freedom and liberty as much as anybody whatsoever; but I must tell you that their liberty and freedom consist in having government, those laws by which their lives and goods may be most their own. It is not their having a share in government; that is nothing appertaining to them. A subject and a sovereign are clean different things; and therefore until you do that—I mean, that you put the people in that liberty—they will never enjoy themselves."[1]

In contemporary plays about Jack Cade and Perkin Warbeck one can see how deep the fear of populism lies in the late sixteenth- and early seventeenth-century audience. Democracy in the Roman plays means mob rule, as in *Julius Caesar* and *Coriolanus.* It means terrorism and violence. It also means autocracy and a succession of autocrats fighting one another to a finish, as in *Antony and Cleopatra.* In the English plays the monarch and in a more shadowy fashion the laws are traditional safeguards against all of this. The safeguards may be breached, but most of the time they remain safeguards. The interconnection of monarch, law, and custom is thus expressed by York in *Richard II:*

> Take Hereford's rights away, and take from Time
> His charters and his customary rights;
> let not to-morrow then ensue to-day;
> Be not thyself; for how art thou a king
> But by fair sequence and succession?
>
> (*R2* II.1.195)

The three Roman plays, *Caesar, Antony and Cleopatra,* and *Coriolanus,* are all concerned with men who are political failures. Their three heroes, Brutus, Antony, and Coriolanus, find a political environment which is intrinsically hostile to their characteristic genius. The nature of their failure, the contrast of what quality they have and what makes for its defeat, became a commentary on the political scene—the politics of their own time and to a significant degree in general.[2] Not only does each of the men fail in his special circumstances; they convince us that they do so for reasons which would certainly make their failure exceedingly likely in any political setting anywhere, anytime, but especially in classical Rome.

Of course *Antony and Cleopatra* stands somewhat apart from the other two. Once upon a time Antony has been a great statesman and a great general. With a part of his mind he is still trying to be so. But he has succumbed to the charms of Cleopatra's brilliant and versatile sexuality. He is, as Enobarbus says, the old lion dying. His remaining blaze of vitality illuminates another sort of achievement, in passion, discovery, and fantasy, different from that to which he has given the rest of his life. His political demise is in part voluntary—in a certain sense of the word. It is in this way that *Antony and Cleopatra* seems to me much less a political play than either the chronicles or *Caesar* and *Coriolanus*. It remains the greatest example of the histrionic fantasy triumphing over factual failure. This is a further reason for placing it where I have in this sequence of essays.

But there is nothing voluntary about the defeat of Brutus and Coriolanus. They are beaten before they start. They are beaten because their personalities are incompatible with the conditions of the political game as it is played in Rome. Theirs are different kinds of incompatibility, but equally destructive. They stand revealed to us by a dramatic analysis of politics that is remorseless and almost objective. They have got the score wrong. It is worth noting that they do not simply aim to live in society, but to dominate and to transform it—the idealistic revolutionary and the messianic soldier. Theirs is a story not just about politics, but politics seen from the angle of a reformer and opponent of an existing system.

Coriolanus's part in the patricio-plebeian struggle belongs to political mythology, and Shakespeare's is one version of it. It is, incidentally, at points different in flavor from Plutarch's. Probably Essex haunts the portrait; possibly the anti-court factions of the first ten years of James I haunt the Tribunes. But Plutarch and his sources render a tolerably realistic and apparently accurate account of the doings in 44–43 B.C., and Shakespeare seems to have clung to this as history pure and simple. Here *Julius Caesar,* reproducing Plutarch closely, is mostly an indisputable picture of the events, in which it is only the characterization of the leading actors in the revolution which is especially Shakespearean.

Both plays seem oddly modern to us. At first it is not quite easy to see why. In our modern world we have no Brutus or

Caesar, and we have fortunately been spared a Coriolanus. I remember having seen two distinguished productions in the thirties, one of *Caesar* by Orson Welles, complete with Sam Browne belts, revolvers, and uniforms, and all the external apparatus of a contemporary fascist state, and one of *Coriolanus* by Hugh Hunt, centered on another sort of charismatic dictator with contemporary overtones. In both cases the attempt to draw together the plays and a definite series of modern events made the productions weaker, not stronger. It is apparently the feeling for politics in these plays, rather than the characters themselves, that makes the plays so modern. Perhaps it is the republican atmosphere, so different from that of real monarchy, that appears familiar to us; perhaps it is the compulsive power of public opinion and its eruption into violence; perhaps it is the force of certain situations which always emerge as the same, however differently proclaimed, making nonsense of the new heaven and new earth which is supposed to follow revolution. It not only repugns Brutus but surprises him to find in Cassius someone who could plead for Lucius Pella, who took bribes:

> . . . shall one of us
> That struck the foremost man of all this world
> But for supporting robbers, shall we now
> Contaminate our fingers with base bribes?
> (*JC* IV.3.21)

We recognize all of this. However, perhaps the reason for our dismayed certainty of the truth of the Roman plays lies somewhere else.

The objective greatness of the history—of these crises in history—has been transformed by the dramatist into something more personal. The defeat at Philippi and Actium and the failure of Coriolanus before Rome are not matters of strategy or moral or philosophical principles. They have become the last stage in the private dreams of their chief actors. These actors make a dramatic move to end their lives, but it is a transforming move, at times a denying move, in the mythical role to which they are committed. Brutus dies like a Roman fool on his own sword, but it is in his imagination that he sees the suicide as a retributive reenactment of his murder of his friend. Coriolanus sacrifices his image of military glory—his very being—and recants to become a "peacemaker" as a sacrifice to the mother who has made him what he is and has never understood her creation. Antony trades off all his attributes as "the greatest prince of the world" (*Ant.* IV.13.54) for his dream of an unlimited sensuality in the next world observed by the admiring ghosts. Even in imagination these acts move before an audience. The personal and the dramatic and their dynamic fusion, what the actor gives to the role when he is at his best and most inspired—this is the final challenge of theater to factual reality; perhaps this is what moves us most in the Roman plays. It is perhaps what we wish for most—a challenge to the drabness of modern politics. The more clear, simple, and brutal these Roman plays are in their rendering of history and politics, the more valuable the challenge, and the more we value it ourselves.

⋘ 5 ⋙

Brutus and Coriolanus:
Political Failures

The key to *Julius Caesar* lies in the relation of the murder to the rest of the play. This is the precipitant of all the issues political and moral of the new Roman state, the state of the triumvirate first and eventually of the Augustan Empire. Yet Shakespeare has read his Roman history, either in Plutarch or otherwise, too well to make Caesar and afterwards Caesar's death a beginning of completely new things. Pompey's statue bleeds at the murder—because indeed Pompey has been Caesar's predecessor and conquered rival. Not so great, not so ultimately authoritative, but already the military man who by his power with the army can dictate to the weakened Senate. Brutus was Pompey's follower, according to Plutarch, because in the rivalry with Caesar he thought Pompey less to blame.[1] The triumvirate comes into existence all too easily for a genuinely new departure from political practice. Shakespeare certainly knew from

Plutarch that a triumvirate of Crassus, Pompey, and Caesar, ten years before the play opens, had similarly kept the con- stitutional government of Rome helpless. The Rome we are looking at is a Rome which has not been a republic, in the old-fashioined way, since Sulla's restoration of it and its sub- sequent failure. Even before that, Sulla and Marius had proved too much for the Optimates to handle.

But, all the same, this is a crucial moment; not that the old republican Rome is going to be restored, but that this is still a time when the old republican sentiment can come naturally on men's lips, together with reflections on the degeneracy of most of those who now called themselves Romans. This is the rhetoric that Cassius specializes in:

> For Romans now
> have thews and sinews like their ancestors;
> but woe the while, our fathers' minds are dead
> and we are govern'd with our mothers' spirits.
> (*JC* I.3.80)

Therefore the lines of Antony's eulogy on the dead Brutus are the more striking.

> All the conspirators, save only he,
> did that they did in envy of great Caesar;
> He, only in a general honest thought
> and common good to all made one of them
> (*JC* V.5.68)

The reference, almost word for word, comes from Plutarch, who quotes Antony to this effect. But there *is* a difference. Shakespeare means Brutus to be singular—Brutus alone on one side and all the conspirators on the other. In the Plutarch

life of Brutus the contrast is invariably between Brutus and
Cassius (with Brutus disinterested and Cassius jealous);
Shakespeare has emphasized the special role of Brutus over
all the others. The conspirators want him because of his an-
cestry, and because of his reputation for disinterestedness,

> O, he sits high in all the people's hearts;
> and that which would appear offence in us
> his countenance, like richest alchemy
> will change to virtue and to worthiness.
>
>   (*JC* I.3.157)

Envy and greed are the usual motives for revolution in
Shakespeare, whether in the chronicle plays or the Roman.
In Brutus he has presented the other element, perhaps generic as he saw it, inside of the classical tradition—that of
the idealist politician which in Rome means devotion to a
dead past, itself supposed to approximate a perfect political
model.

The play certainly emphasizes the note of envy in the rest
of the opposition. It is not only the eloquence of Cassius;
there is the sourness and disappointed hatred of Casca to
deepen the color. Casca hates everybody—Caesar for being
Caesar, but certainly no less his honest neighbors who "utter'd such a deal of stinking breath . . . [that] for mine own
part, I durst not laugh for fear of opening my lips and receiving the bad air" (I.2.245). Perhaps he is "quick mettle" still,
as Cassius asserts, somewhere underneath, but one is somewhat more inclined to feel sympathetic to Antony's later description of him:

> Whilst damned Casca, like a cur, behind
> Struck Caesar on the neck.
>
>   (*JC* V.1.43)

There is Caius Ligarius, who also has obligations to Caesar, but who also in a sinister way rejoices over the need of the plot "to make some sick that now are whole."

The envy is directed against the autocracy of Caesar.

> Why, man, he doth bestride the narrow world
> like a Colossus, and we petty men
> walk under his huge legs, and peep about
> to find ourselves dishonorable graves.
>   (*JC* I.2.135)

It is the blend of Brutus's archaic republicanism with Cassius's intense (and, according to Plutarch, intensely personal) jealousy which makes them the natural leaders of the conspirators. Both are against the predominance of anyone in authority. Cassius very cunningly blurs the line between his own personal motives and Brutus's highly theoretical ones in the lines . . .

> but, for my single self,
> I had as lief not be as live to be
> in awe of such a thing as I myself
>   (*JC* I.2.95)

—which could rate as old Roman democracy or resentment at any natural superior. But at some level Brutus always knows that Cassius is seducing him from some truly felt loyalty. "Since Cassius first did whet me against Caesar," he says, "I have not slept" (*JC* II.1.62). Cassius himself speaks of his own actions quite unequivocally.

> Well, Brutus, thou are noble; yet I see
> thy honorable mettle maybe wrought

> from that it is dispos'd: therefore it is meet
> that noble minds keep ever with their likes;
> For who so firm that cannot be seduc'd?
> Caesar doth bear me hard but he loves Brutus.
>
> *(JC* I.2.308)

Many critics have noticed the similarity of Cassius's temptation of Brutus and that of Macbeth by his wife. Both those
assailed have their weak spots, their inchoate dissatisfactions
and ambitions which are played on. Brutus's description of
his own condition is certainly very like that of Macbeth.

> Between the acting of a dreadful thing
> and the first motion, all the interim is
> like a phantasma or a hideous dream.
>
> *(JC* II.1.63)

Yet this Roman version of the temptation is very subtle—for
it is different. Brutus is being tempted to murder a friend and
the head of the Roman state—but hardly his liege lord and
sovereign. The dictator is the holder of power unsanctified,
though its illegality lies only in the contrast between the ex-
ternals of the republican authority and the spirit of the office
as Caesar conceives it. All the same, this is 44 B.C., and the
republic has long been at the disposal of soldiers who became
republican magistrates by pressure and retain the office by
pressure, too. Brutus knew this situation well under Pompey. The final step, which seems to make the decisive difference, would be the assumption of the one title—king—so
obnoxious to the Roman republican traditions. Even without
this new insult to the past, Caesar still remains the sole
holder of effective legal power in Rome. What Brutus wants
to do is to turn the clock back to an ideal condition of lib-

erty—which was represented, within any Roman historical period at all near this one, by a close-knit oligarchy of aristocratic families.

In the play, I believe, it is clear that Brutus is wrong in his principles, that is, justice does not necessarily stand on his side of the case; Caesar is hardly, even technically, an illegal magistrate; he is hardly an illegal magistrate at all in terms of immediate historical precedent. Brutus is also very often wrong in his practical judgment—as in allowing Antony to speak at Caesar's funeral. Antony's eulogy of Brutus after death is couched in conventional and really formal terms. There are Brutus's principles, yes; there is his disinterestedness. How much are they worth to our sympathy or antipathy in the historical scale, as the play conveys measurement? It is only his character that bears him with dignity and decency through a series of foolish and practically unjustifiable actions. For Shakespeare, as the stage setter for this drama of classical political life, is not on the side of the sentimental republican tradition as seen by men like Tacitus or by a Greek provincial literateur like Plutarch (both living one and two centuries after any effective republican government had ended); nor even, I suspect, is he sympathetic with the temporizing and compromising political blindness of the contemporary Cicero. To all of these as sources, he would, one way or another, have ready access. No doubt he used the easiest and most popular versions he could get, and perhaps all the sources came to him simply through North's Plutarch. The events of the last half of the last century B.C. are being seen through the eyes of an early seventeenth-century Englishman who can hardly have felt that Caesar's aspiration to the title of king puts him beyond the bounds of ordinary political decency. Nor his concentration of authority to nearly absolute proportions. But the power struggles which the murder of Caesar occasioned and the subsequent civil war are a real terror to an Englishman who lived in the shadow of the Wars of the Roses and under the apprehensions of the doubtful transference of the Crown from Elizabeth to James I.

This is my summing up of the most obvious facts of Shakespeare's approach to classical republican (Roman) history. But after all, it is the play that convinces—and one would have thought that the weight of the play shows certainly Brutus as the political fool who occasioned a great deal of suffering. The play does show that; but there has been a determined effort among the critics to make us think that it carries overtones of admiration for the tragedy of the Roman republic, in its last days, which Brutus defended and tried to revive. I do not think it does. What it carries is an extraordinary study of the nature of the man who was the champion of this idealistic republicanism. What it does further is to present the whole Roman scene with a kind of realism which disperses the fog of public-relations history. Thus we see, apart from Brutus, a horrible mob, a feeble and vain elderly dictator—the best thing to say for him being that he is not inclined to hurt anyone anymore—a crew of clever adventurers—Antony, Octavian, and (on the conspirators' side) Cassius—and a stupid adventurer, Lepidus. Such portraits are inspired by prodigious imaginative penetration of classical political life; perhaps it is simply true to the historical reality in Rome somehow grasped by genius, perhaps projected out of a kinship with late sixteenth-century European history; certainly it is true to some inherent political sense of the most general kind.

The character of Brutus is all important in *Julius Caesar* both as it affects his own tragedy and the tragedy of Rome in those years. In very simple outline the tragedy is his—because he killed his friend, his ruin is brought about by the ghost of the dead man. (It is the Senecan model, but of course made immensely more subtle.) But the tragedy is Rome's because, on his participation, indeed on his leadership, depend the assassination and the revolution, and the course it took to its own destruction. The usual guidelines, which Shakespeare deliberately calls in question, are the solid merit of Brutus personally as Stoic philosopher and publicly as a champion of liberty. The contravention is deliberate because the atmosphere of the play is as far removed as possible from a classical "model." It is entirely human and alive. As *Troilus and Cressida* shows the relation between living reality and stereotypes of epic (as Shakespeare saw it)—in a spirit of black comedy, this play shows the relation between a strictly traditional view of a great historical event, where the roles are readily identifiable with perfect models, and the actual thing. But it is no black comedy. It is not extravagant or grotesque. It is poetic description of a supreme political moment, in the sparest poetical terms. It is indeed a stripped-down poetry and stripped-down politics.

The poetry and prose employed by Brutus yield a curious commentary on his mentality. A friend once called my attention to the peculiar fact that it is only in the Forum speech that Brutus employs prose. Even in the dialogue with Cassius and Casca, Brutus's speeches seem all readable as blank verse. Those prose speeches in the Forum sit very ill on him. They are to the last degree mannered and stiff: "Hear me for my cause, and be silent that you may hear. Believe me for mine honour, and have respect to mine honour, that you may believe" (*JC* III.2.13). That is certainly not the way to impress that crowd. "Friends, Romans, countrymen, lend me your ears! I come to bury Caesar, not to praise him" is the right way. Apparently prose is not Brutus's natural way of communicating. *That* is blank verse, with the formulization of rhythms and cadences. There we have the habitual Brutus with music and shape to his words, that come from an accepted norm which has become a part of him. It is of course the "norm" for all the characters at most moments throughout the play. Brutus clearly feels that his speech to the crowd must be something special. He therefore tries to establish a formalization of his own, with the result that he sounds pedantic and artificial. He is in general shy and rather inarticulate. In his poetry he is for the most part a very quiet presence without extreme emphasis on striking phrases. To take a few examples where we might expect something different.

> "Speak, strike, redress!" Am I entreated
> To speak, and strike? O Rome, I make thee promise,
> If the redress will follow, thou receiv'st
> Thy full petition at the hand of Brutus!
>
> (*JC* II.1.55)

At times of emotion indeed he tends to *reduce* the tempo.

> Into what dangers would you lead me, Cassius,
> That you would have me seek into myself
> For that which is not in me?
>
> (*JC* I.2.63)

But at his deepest, and most often in soliloquy, where the nakedness of the phrase moves directly into solemnity without any communication with colloquialism, he expresses himself in moving (and most economical) poetry.

> It must be by his death; and for my part,
> I know no personal cause to spurn at him,

But for the general. He would be crown'd:
How that might change his nature, there's the
    question.
It is the bright day that brings forth the adder;
and that craves wary walking.

$$(JC \text{ II.1.10})$$

Sometimes his fundamental honesty sets on his poetry to make war on the verbal formulae with which he tries to control the violence of life.

Let us be sacrificers, but not butchers, Caius.
We all stand up against the spirit of Caesar;
And in the spirit of men there is no blood:
O then that we could come by Caesar's spirit,
And not dismember Caesar! But, alas!
Caesar must bleed for it! And, gentle friends,
Let's kill him boldly, but not wrathfully;
Let's carve him as a dish fit for the gods,
Not hew him as a carcass fit for hounds:

$$(JC \text{ II.1.166})$$

Here the basic conceit is lamentably artificial and dishonest— the "removal" of Caesar in spirit without injuring the body. But Brutus cannot conceal from his mind's eye what the act is really like. It is the likeness of the huntsman feeding his hounds with a carrion carcass ("flesh" for the dogs) because it was not fit for meat and had to be destroyed. The men cut flesh from bone carelessly—"hew"; the meat is worthless except for animals. Compare the strength of this picture with the literary "carve him a dish fit for the gods." Indeed Brutus's greatest weakness is his determination to make all political situations conform to a mental formula which comes to him in a ready-made verbalization. For instance, here he is, speaking to the conspirators as they make their formal association.

No, not an oath! if not the face of men,
The sufferance of our souls, the time's abuse,—
If these be motives weak, break off betimes,
And every man hence to his idle bed; . . .

(JC II.1.114)

That is a stale sentiment, in tired language. Of Cicero:

. . . let us not break with him;
For he will never follow anything
That other men begin.

(JC II.1.150)

Another ready-made phrase. Of Cassius's suggestion that they should execute Antony:

Cass: I think it is not meet,
Mark Antony, so well beloved of Caesar,
Should outlive Caesar.

(JC II.1.155)

Bru: Our course will seem too bloody, Caius Cassius,
To cut the head off and then hack the limbs

(JC II.1.162)

—the metaphor has taken the place of thought. Yet the last instance is also part of Shakespeare's realistic portrait. Brutus is the type of idealistic revolutionary[2] (do we remember that in his last moments Antony, in *Antony and Cleopatra,* claims as his merit—"And 'twas I that the *mad* Brutus ended?" [*Ant.* III.9.37]). Yet there are things he will not do in violation of humanity, no matter what the needs of his idealistic program. He can just bring himself to kill Caesar, disregarding his obligations to the man—perhaps because his obligations force him to think of a dichotomy of friendship and duty, and of course duty wins. He can disregard also his uncomfortable sense of Caesar's objective innocence in comparison with his potential mischief.

> since the quarrel
> will bear no colour for the thing he is,
> fashion it thus: that what he is, augmented,
> would run to these and these extremities;
> and therefore think him as a serpent's egg
> which, hatch'd, would as his kind grow mischievous
> and kill him in the shell
>
> (*JC* II.1.28)

But he will not carry this form of reasoning to the length of murdering Antony. Much less could he be induced to the wholesale execution of one hundred potential "dangers" to the newly established order—which his rivals, the mercurial Antony, the estimable Octavian, and the dull plodder Lepidus, so lightheartedly engage in ("Look, with a spot I damn him!" [*JC* IV1.6.]). He is in truth the "gentle" Brutus; he probably speaks the truth of himself when he says,

> O Cassius, you are yoked with a lamb
> That carries anger as the flint bears fire
> Who much enforced, shows a hasty spark,
> and straight is cold again.
>
> (*JC* IV.3.109)

The latter part of the play shows Brutus aware that he has lost his guidelines—and his certainty—in this new world of proscriptions by his rivals and bribery and corruption by his friends. He says to Pindarus, Cassius's man, "Your master has given me cause to wish things done, undone." In the end it is toward expiation he is moving. His personal offense must be paid for.

> Night hangs upon my eyes; my bones would rest
> that have but labour'd to attain this hour.
> > (*JC* V.5.41)

We can well believe his last words, as he runs on his sword.

> "Caesar, now be still;
> I killed not thee with half so good a will."
> > (*JC* V.5.50)

Both Brutus and Coriolanus are drawn into politics by others, to deal with special contingencies. They are both, in a sense, an engine in the hands that try to manipulate them. (The word engine is actually used of Coriolanus in his final approach to Rome, but it is then out of control.) Once the special contingency is past, the engine turns out not to be particularly suitable for more general political purposes. Cassius lived to regret Brutus's direction of the plot: thanks to Brutus, Antony is not only alive but manages the funeral of Caesar. Brutus is also responsible for the mistake in strategy which gives Antony the victory in the last battle. These are typical mistakes on Brutus's part; they are expressions of his inelasticity of mind. But Coriolanus is dangerous to those who employ him as Brutus never would be. For what is being harnessed in Coriolanus's case is an immense personal energy and a distorted temperament—in the person of a brilliant soldier. It is not his intellectual convictions that are the difficulty or stumbling block, as with Brutus. It is the individual power of a man utterly uncontrollable by those who would employ him. In military terms, it is hardly his tactical or strategic gifts that win him his distinction. It is his inhuman bravery and his ability, with the right sort of followers, to draw them after him like a magnet. It is no accident that he shows at his best when second in command to Cominius. But inside of the Roman state, as described by Plutarch and taken over by Shakespeare—and indeed perhaps in all the Shakespearean historical-political plays—soldiers must also be politicians to achieve final success. In this case the Roman nobles try to make Coriolanus a politician as well as a soldier, with disastrous results to themselves and himself.

Shakespeare has several times touched on the story of the soldier employed by his country for her salvation and then ungratefully discarded. There are echoes of the situation in Othello. Brabantio has lost his suit to the Duke before he started, because the state then needs Othello against the Turk. When, after the Turk's defeat Othello is superseded in favor of Cassio, it *may* only be Othello's jealousy, on the other grounds, which makes this so bitter. But Lodovico at least thinks it natural that Othello should be annoyed, implying that the recall may properly be viewed as a degradation. His moment of value is past. In *Timon of Athens,* Alcibiades is the general who is exactly in Coriolanus's position; and he finally makes the Athenian Senate submit. But the significant feature, the ungratefulness of the country and the revenge of the general, is only vestigially there in *Othello,* and the character of the general is not really developed in *Timon.* In *Coriolanus* the action—from service to the opportunity of re-

venge to the rejection of revenge—is there; and the character
is central to the play.

Two quotations lie at the heart of the understanding of
Coriolanus. The first is in the mouth of the officer who is
preparing the scene for the candidates for consulship. He is
speaking of Coriolanus's attitude to the people whose votes
he is soliciting. "If he did not care whether he had their love
or no, he waved indifferently 'twixt doing them neither good
nor harm; but he seeks their hate with greater devotion than
they can render it him and leaves nothing undone that may
fully discover him their opposite. Now, to seem to affect the
malice and displeasure of the people is as bad as that which
he dislikes, to flatter them for their love" (*Cor.* II.2.18). The
second is spoken by his Volscian rival Aufidius, and covers
not only his character but the progress throughout the action.

> I think he'll be to Rome
> as is the osprey to the fish, who takes it
> by sovereignty of nature. First he was
> a noble servant to them, but he could not
> carry his honors even. Whether twas pride
> which out of daily fortune ever taints
> the happy man; whether defect of judgement,
> to fail in the disposing of those chances
> which he was lord of; or whether nature
> not to be other than one thing, not moving
> from the casque to the cushion, but commanding
>   peace
> even with the same austerity and garb
> as he controll'd the war; but one of these
> (as he hath spices of them all, not all,
> for I dare so far free him) made him fear'd

> so hated and so banished; but he has a merit
> to choke it in the utterance.
>
> (*Cor.* IV.7.33)

The first quotation registers the sense of Coriolanus's perversity in his attitude toward the people. The second introduces the enigmatic side of his career of misfortune. The typical expression of the career is explosive and violent. The dialogue with the tribunes after the candidacy for the consulship and the treason trial both bear the same marks. Moreover, it is this which ensures that Coriolanus meets his end, not with the dignity and drama of self-sacrifice, as he parts from his mother, but petulantly, driven to fury by Aufidius's taunt, "boy of tears." He is someone whose breaking point is unpredictable but painfully near the surface; he cannot control his reactions to a predetermined end. In Aufidius's catalogue of the defects which ruined him, we notice that conceit and misjudgment (apparent enough) give place as a solution of the puzzle of his failure to a more interesting possibility: that something in him, peculiarly his own, is tied to being a soldier. He cannot transform this gift to the purposes of peace without carrying along what amounts to the gestures and manners of his natural profession, "commanding peace with the same austerity and garb as war." It is ironic, in the light of this, to see that Coriolanus's death occurs in the enterprise which he himself describes:

> Though I cannot make true wars
> I'll frame convenient peace.
>
> (*Cor.* V.3.190)

The achievement of the Shakespearean portrait is that we finally understand the man—through his relation to his mother, to his son, and through the description of the cold and sticky traps set for him. The greatness of the creation, for us, is that without awakening in us ordinary sympathy (such as, for instance, we feel intensely for Othello or Hamlet), his destruction implies for us the meaningful loss of something admirable and extraordinary. The why of the perversity which the officer mentions is never spelled out; there is no conjuring away the character of Coriolanus with notes on his mental immaturity. What we see is illumination, not explanation.[3] He will not allow any value other than his own. The people exist as a dull neutral threat to his self-assertion. They and their manipulators are like a bog in which he sticks. So he tries to force them into actual enmity, which is something he understands. The balanced estimate is Aufidius's. Coriolanus is proud, with poor practical judgment, a genius as a soldier and a fool at most other things. He has spices of all of these defects, but it is not their combination that ruins him. It is one of them; that one is certainly the third. It is the singleness of his genius that does him down. The play makes clear why it was only soldiership that makes him feel himself; it is why the tests other than military ones automatically are impossible for him.

Coriolanus in his dialogue with his mother after the debacle of the treason trial:

> *Cor.*   I muse my mother
>   does not approve me further, who was wont
>   to call them woolen vassals . . .
>
>   (*Cor.* III.2.7)

Volumnia *enters.*

>   I talk of you:
>   why did you wish me milder? Would you have me

> false to my nature? Rather say, I play
> The man I am . . .

> *Vol.*   You might have been enough the man you are
>   with striving less to be so.
>
> > (*Cor.* III.2.19)

But Coriolanus's nature demands an exhibition, a histrionic creation for his sentiments and emotions before they can correspond with what he owns as his. But his mother misunderstands. She takes "the man you are" as an underlying static thing, in favor of which much else, including deception, may be consciously practiced. For him neither sentiments nor acts are satisfactory unless they receive a shape drawn from the theater. It is not for nothing that, when finally confronted first by his wife and then his mother, as he storms toward the gates of Rome, he says,

> Like a dull actor now,
> I have forgot my part, and I am out
> Even to a full disgrace.
>
> > (*Cor.* V.3.40)

What he refers to is, of course, not simply "going up on his lines." It is the loss of the certainty of his stage personality. A few minutes before, he had invoked this proper role:

> Let the Volsces
> plough Rome and harrow Italy; I'll never
> be such a gosling to obey instinct, but stand
> as if a man were author of himself
> and knew no other kin.
>
> > (*Cor.* V.3.33)

When his horrible son had his encounter with the butterfly, Valeria describes it thus: "I saw him run after a gilded butterfly, and when he caught it, he let it go again, and after it again, and over and over he comes, and up again; catch'd it again; or whether his fall enrag'd him, or how 'twas, he did so set his teeth and tear it. O, I warrant, how he mammock'd it" (*Cor.* I.3.60). This is a youthful version of the father, failing to discover the proper drama to express what he felt. Coriolanus throughout the play constantly tries to find an appropriate role for the raw material of his emotion and ambition. "I cannot prove false to my nature" (which would be acting as a pretense). "I play the man I am" (when I reject in extravagant but controlled terms the rights the electorate has over me). When he once is driven to accept the formality of the suppliant's posture in the candidature, he will assume the dress, but he will not show the scars. The robe of humility becomes his actor's dress. It can be made to accord with the highly stylized sarcasm with which he "begs the honest voices." The scars will not do, because they are inarticulate and cannot be disguised. They are of his flesh; a true actor may manifest even these, but then he must involve himself more with the sensitivities of his particular audience than Coriolanus cares to do.[4]

In the heat of the battle Coriolanus remembers the poor man of Corioli who had given him hospitality, as he hears him call for help. An obligation such as this is sacred to Coriolanus because he wishes to owe nothing to anyone. So he asks Cominius to save the man—which the commander agrees to do. Unfortunately, although Coriolanus remembers the obligation, he was never enough aware of the person to whom he is obliged to recollect his name. Absolute autarchy, absolute autonomy, absolute voluntariness. This is what Coriolanus wishes. He objects nearly as much to the decorations given him by his aristocratic peers as to the begging of votes from the Commons which is forced on him. No act of his seems to him clean and decent unless he is entirely on the giving side. If there is a reward for him, it all becomes a process, the other end of which lies in someone else's hand.

In dealing with the contingencies which are inevitable for a military commander serving in high posts, he has evolved a series of acts and attitudes which express himself adequately to himself—as they express that self to the audience. In fact his patriotism and his devotion to his aristocratic class are only skin deep. The one crumples when his country wrongs him; the other disappears so completely that he can confuse friends and foes in the general mass of those who have wronged him. His audience is an ideal audience—the perfect warriors, the perfect aristocrats, the perfect country. I am inclined to add also, the perfect mother. But the perfect society of warriors turns into the crafty politician Aufidius, the perfect aristocrats into the shrewdly temporizing Menenius, the perfect fatherland into an uneasy combination of a manipulative political machine and a dull, vicious electorate. And the perfect mother has so little notion of the man she has created that she fails entirely to understand that pretense of any sort is impossible for him—since such pretense implies that he is afraid of someone or wants someone to give him something which they would not do unsolicited; any such idea makes the act nearly an emotional impossibility for Coriolanus. Volumnia thrusts him into the effort for the consulship, and then into the pleading at the treason trial. Both times the role, for which he is cast, breaks down through the spontaneous ill will of the other actor in the act. For Coriolanus has nothing to buttress him, as soon as some difficulty in communication or cordiality spontaneously appears. He is forced by his mother's persuasions to try to pretend; but there is no inward acquiescence in the part: he is not performing as the true actor would, by yielding himself to the personality which he is projecting. Therefore it can be upset at any moment.

In only one sphere can Coriolanus allow of the elastic compromise, which is ordinary life—and that, at least according to Volumnia, is in war. War for Coriolanus, one imagines, is mostly to be like the struggle for Corioli—a desperate affair of hand-to-hand combat. But he can apparently at times also see a strategy. Volumnia says:

> I have heard you say
> honour and policy, like unsevered friends
> in war do grow together; grant that, and tell me
> in peace what each of them by th' other lose
> that they combine not there.
>
> > (*Cor.* III.2.41)

But in war the object is not his own aggrandizement, or the loss simply that of his own life. It is a game, and as a stylized game it is Coriolanus's special interest, a perfect mimic representation of the perfect life. But to flatter to make himself consul, to defend himself from the malice and tactics of the Tribunes—clearly that is to infract "the man he is" in the "playing" of that resplendent being.

This last test of him—when Volumnia overrules him before the gates of Rome, when he seeks his last and most glorious role

> He was a kind of nothing, titleless,
> till he had forged himself a name o' the fire
> of burning Rome . . .
>
> > (*Cor.* V.1.13)

is different from the others. Before, he had yielded to her, and tried to be what she wanted him to be, acknowledging implicitly the full correctness of her judgments. But this time he knows she is sending him to his destruction—and he still yields. It is now a conscious act of sacrifice, the final strange act of self-abnegation by this egotist.

> O my mother, mother! O!
> you have won a happy victory to Rome;
> but, for your son, believe it,—O believe it—
> most dangerously you have with him prevail'd
> if not most mortal to him . . .
>
> (*Cor.* V.3.185)

It is a special note in the play's reality that it does not end like this—which would be a satisfactory gesture in the Coriolanus vein—but in the miserable squabble between him and Aufidius, and in the assassination which had been planned to arise from it.

Both Brutus and Coriolanus are men whose private and personal qualities are sought by others for political purposes, and their political employment destroys them. Very often it is the reputation for the quality rather than the quality itself that is wanted. It is Brutus's value as a disinterested, old-fashioned Roman that makes him desirable to the conspirators. Really it is Brutus as a talking-point that matters. It is Coriolanus's value as a soldier that makes the aristocrats wish for his consulship, but it is certainly also the elaborate hero worship so tellingly and malignantly described by the Tribunes, his enemies, and by the Senate, his friends, that makes him, from the point of view of those friends, the proper man for the head of the state.

It is peculiarly the extreme of virtue in the private man, or at least his reputation for that extreme of virtue, that is sought after for his public function. Yet it is certain that the aspirations and theories of the selected victim will, then, be most in conflict with the grimy reality of politics. For instance, that grimy reality, both in the English chronicles and in the Roman plays, turns a great deal on speechmaking, public and private, but the true nature of politics involves a habitual discrepancy between such announced sentiments and what lies behind them. To take two examples. In *Henry V* we open with a conversation between two prominent churchmen concerned with Henry's attitude toward church taxation. For the Church, everything, we are told, depends on whether the king will tax the church as many of his subjects would have him, or spare it. Taxation would be utter ruin. The next scene shows us Henry solemnly consulting these church dignitaries on his claim to the throne of France. In his adjuration the king urges the archbishops to examine their consciences at depth. Their uttermost scruple must be given rein; they must strain nothing in order to win the royal approbation. Only the solemn truth about the Salic Law, as they saw it, will do. We are hardly surprised that Henry is confirmed in his claim, though all we have to go on is the ironic juxtaposition of our knowlege of the archbishops before the consultation with the king and after it.

In a way, Antony's address to the crowd at Caesar's funeral is only a blown-up version of the whole art of political rhetoric in its more democratic manifestations. It is Antony's subtle movement from tributes to Brutus to his attack upon him that gives the speech its meaning—and the meaning is a knife in the back.

> Yet Brutus says he was ambitious,
> and sure he is an honorable man.

> I speak not to disprove what Brutus spoke
> but here I am to speak what I do know.
> You all did love him once, not without cause,
> What cause withholds you then to mourn for
>   him?

(JC III.2.98)

Successful politics for Shakespeare is a place where any theory of human rights or man's place in the universe or any efforts toward objective truth or even any intensity of personal integrity exists only as a facade from behind which one can talk. The realities are greed, ambition, envy, hatred, and contempt. This is true without exception in the English plays, the Roman and the fictionalized plays with a Ruritanian or mythological background. The pursuit of power is sordid and its devotees sordid. These men themselves, the power seekers, are only rarely even sizeable. The definition of distinction either in quality or in character, except in a great criminal like Macbeth, tends to exclude the true power seeker. In fact it is *against* politics, in the ordinary sense of the word, that the definition of such distinction is framed.

Measure for Measure:
Mythological History, Reality, and the Stage

In the person of Prince Hal, in the two parts of *Henry IV,* Shakespeare has formally given over some of the action to a kind of stage director, within the play. But in *Measure for Measure* the stage play is geared both to its own staginess and its representation of law-in-politics and political reform. It is just that Angelo should be surrendered to Mariana as her "husband." It is equally just, and also funny, that she should then surrender him to the chopping block for his crimes. The play which the Duke-reformer-director directs turns out to be black comedy, ironic and thoroughly unsympathetic humanly. In its mood and its peculiar form it reveals a way of seeing law and its logic and the relation of ethics and politics that nothing else in Shakespeare does.

Suppose a Master Puppeteer with absolute power (perhaps less absolute power than the absolute knack of appearing at the right moment) could put a different and good end to projected disaster. What would you the audience think of that, if you had entirely entered into the complicated, limited, mixed-up world of human reality to start with? And suppose that he arranged the proper "they lived happily every after" in strictly legal terms so that humorous but logical trials for everyone would complement their human sufferings at the beginning (e.g., Mariana is offered her reluctant suitor as husband and after the marriage is asked to surrender him directly to execution as a criminal). How would this look as a commentary on ethics and law? And finally after the Master Joker has made the two proper marriages—the boy and girl who went to bed together before marriage, the official and his betrothed, whom he did *not* want to go to bed with but was tricked into doing so—what is left but to arrange the marriage of the Master Joker himself to that solemn bit of ascetic virtue, the ex-novice Isabella? And what would you think of that? And after all maybe, as the final humbugging mysterious question, what would you think the Master Joker himself was, in his role of hypothetical magician? This, I submit, is what *Measure for Measure* is asking us. It is an "asking" play, its characteristic form a probing of the audience's response, with a final answer perhaps mischievously withheld.

One can hardly call much of *Measure for Measure* great poetry. Yet it *has* passages of extraordinary poetry; moreover, their very sporadic occurrence and their own power force our attention to some peculiar share they must possess toward its interpretation. They start out from the page, they force one's attention to themselves as they fall from the actor's lips. They must be special signals to be heeded, in some sense charting the course for the meaning of the whole.

> *Claudio:*
> As surfeit is the father of much fast,

So every scope by the immoderate use
Turns to restraint. Our natures do pursue,
Like rats that ravin down their proper bane,
A thirsty evil, and when we drink we die.

(*MM* I.2.125)

Claudio:
Ay, but to die, and go we know not where;
to lie in cold obstruction, and to rot;
This sensible warm motion to become
A kneaded clod; and the delighted spirit
To bathe in fiery floods.

(*MM* III.1.117)

Isabella:
Why all the souls that were were forfeit once,
And He that might the vantage best have took
Found out the remedy.

(*MM* II.2.73)

Isabella:
But man, proud man,
Dressed in a little brief authority,
Most ignorant of what he's most assured
(His glassy essence) like an angry ape
Plays such fantastic tricks before high heaven
As make the angels weep; who, with our spleens,
Would all themselves laugh mortal.

(*MM* II.2.117)

Angelo:
But it is I,
That, lying by the violet in the sun,

Do as the carrion does, not as the flow'r,
Corrupt with virtuous season.

(MM II.2.165)

There are more such passages—but not many. Almost anyone reading the play, or even more seeing it, will pick out these same passages and afterwards will not be able to extend the list much. With the possible exception of Angelo's image of the flower and the carrion, they are not especially characteristic of the speaker. But they are rooted in the immediacy of a moment impinging on a certain character. They are notable also as images, which reach beyond their context and dominate us. The rats drinking after their poison, the monkey playing before the mirror, create a truth for us; the images have seized and frozen a moment of passionate insight. Their luminous impermanence lies at the heart of the play. Moreover, together, they seem to constitute a kind of ethical commentary the more telling because its positive content (in the way of directive) is very little. It emphasizes, rather, an abstention from judgment, a passive recognition of man's fallibility, a passive recognition of his need for forgiveness, a passive recognition of his sensual and bodily corruption. The one really positive conclusion is that one should not judge, because self-examination always reveals traits one possesses in common with the criminal. This is indeed the deduction drawn from what the Duke himself, Isabella, and Escalus say at their most sincere. But the Duke hardly stops there, as the magnetic passages I have quoted do.

He who the sword of heaven will bear
Should be as holy as severe . . .

(MM III.2.262)

is more than a satiric commentary on the falsity of Angelo. It sketches the Duke's hope for a positively superior ruler. "Be absolute for death" is intended to be a help to the unfortunate Claudio. One realizes gradually that the position of the Duke is that of an ideal lawgiver, even if he is now posing as the intelligent amateur. Perhaps this is a part of the Duke, who is "One that above all other strifes, contended especially to know himself" (*MM* III.2.232), as Escalus says. But he is bent on translating this knowledge into a social prescription for justice and rule for other men. The flickering ironic light of the play bears on the improbability or impossibility of reconciling these two things—the complex truth of the inner personal reaction and the simplified administrative prescription that grows out of it.

The poetic passages on our list seem to stretch the imaginative grasp of the speakers to the uttermost, beyond their ordinary stage personality or the direct needs of the situation. Claudio in his misery finds himself and Juliet in extreme danger of their lives. In his thoughts, appetite, liberty, and repression take on this lurid image of the thirsty rats. The image is potent—lust as the direct and relentless incentive to death. It is a pathological view of nature—the succession of extremes. To us, it connects with the syphilis jokes earlier in the play, and with the explicit conjunction of death house and whorehouse and hangman and bawd in the later part. But the Claudio who sees this is certainly not the Claudio of cooler moments, nor is it his personal case which truly provokes this comment. It is Vienna, the city of pathological extremes in succession, dubbed on to the whole of nature. Claudio knows that his own is scarcely more than a technical infraction of chastity, even legally speaking; certainly no example of ravening lust. His devastating comment is rooted only in the rather frigid conceit of the contrast of his present "restraint," that is, fetters, and his previous "license." But his moment of terror drives him to see something which creates a truth for us and for him in the thirst-driven rats. The poetry has attained a complicated richness of meaning beyond the man's reasoned understanding and the requirements of the situation. So also with "Aye, but to die and go we know not where." This is Claudio's answer to his own previous acquiescence in the Duke's "be absolute for death." As long as death was not actual the excellent reasoning of the Duke stands firm. When Claudio sees some chance, however unpleasant, of escaping, the sense of life and its loss becomes fervent. But

> This sensible warm motion to become
> A kneaded clod

is something special. It is a dimension of truth not reached in the Duke's philosophizing, even in the deeper and more particular bits such as the description of life as "an after dinner sleep"; Claudio's phrases create a generalization about the condition of being alive, and the imagination of being dead, totally flavored by the immediacy of one man's feelings. Such a transfusion of the general by personal experience, the uniqueness in the midst of generalization, wars in advance on the legal fictions of the latter part of the play—put forward in whatever mocking mood—concerning the swapping indifferently of men's heads and women's bodies. And it does set off the proper air of black comedy and superficial lightheartedness of those fictions.

Nothing puts before us with such clarity Angelo's offense as the carrion and the flower, in juxtaposition, under the equally warming rays of the sun—the rotting of the flesh, the opening of the flower. It is the temptation of Isabella, the newly discovered want of self-control, even of enlightened self-interest, that staggers him out of his customary mold. We never see him with such a moment of self-knowledge again. The play does not need him in that way. Again, the carrion and the flower under the sun is an image that dominates our reception of the rest of the play. It is a kind of summing up (and transforming) of our scattered impressions from Lucio, Isabella, the gentlemen in the "King of Hungary" scene, Mrs. Overdone and Pompey. The opportunity to be what he wants, afforded Angelo by the Duke's allowance, shows the dark side of the ascetic, in the delight in cruelty as the flavoring of his passion for Isabella. The flesh which is a simple and funny component of humanity for Lucio, The Enemy for Isabella, the object of trade for the bawds and brothel keepers, and the terror of the victims of syphilis receives its definitive poetic shape in the rotting carrion beside the flower as the sun warms both. This is how, truly enough, Angelo sees himself in his new license.

No one will forget Isabella's image of the monkey before the mirror climaxed by the ambiguous phrase "His glassy essence." This too dominates the play, for it includes, along with the general class of officeholders, denounced by Isabella, much of the Duke's acts, his formalized efforts toward retribution, the sermons he delivers as Friar, the self-righteous legalism of Angelo—and even the holiness of the thing "enskied and sainted" that is Isabella herself.

> Most ignorant of what he's most assured,
> (His glassy essence) . . .

Isabella does indeed feel the truth of

> Why all the souls that were were forfeit once
> And He that might the advantage best have took
> Found out the remedy.

But it is hard to think that mercy and tolerance of man's weaknesses and sins are the mainspring of her disposition or that her Christ is predominantly one of forgiveness. True, later she does forgive Angelo; she even pleads for him at Mariana's request. But on that occasion her arguments show the Isabella we believe in—and not very much the girl of the reference to the forgiving Christ. This is the Isabella who insists that the important thing is that Claudio her brother did copulate with Juliet and is therefore guilty of his offense before the law; whereas Angelo did not do so with herself, even though he tried to, and thought he had.

For all its ambiguities, and its insights anchored in moments, this play is undeniably authoritative. It forces us to believe, however mysteriously, that it is the expression of a peculiarly sophisticated truth. What that truth is, which comprehends such a range of approaches to it as are comprised in the attitudes of Angelo, Escalus, the Duke, Isabella, and even Lucio and Pompey, what the meaning is of the conflicts among the approaches, that is what everyone (and not only critics), have looked for in *Measure for Measure*. The play moves us, involves us in the fate of its characters, but it is the underlying meaning, which weaves together all, that holds our concern, the vantage point from which we must survey the whole thing. This is as true in the theater as in the study. There are all sorts of Dukes in the critical tradition, all sorts of Isabellas. There are champions of the play as a Christian fable—and there are certainly heavily Christian overtones. There are Dukes and Isabellas who are hypocrites both. Dover Wilson is so dissatisfied that he has recourse to the theory of an entirely corrupted text made of an incomplete version left by Shakespeare and somehow later fudged into shape.[1]

The realism of *Measure for Measure*—for in a sense realism

one must call it—is peculiar. The Duke and his project for
Vienna indeed look as though they had stepped out of a fable.
Some of the names—Froth, Elbow, Mrs. Overdone—are
broad comic allegory. Isabella and Claudio, Juliet, Mariana,
even Angelo himself are skeleton figures. Yet we are drawn
into the plot, as though it said something of an easily recognizable realistic world. The play is continually suggesting a
serious and most unpleasant side. Claudio's risk of death,
Angelo's cruelty and perfidy, penetrates us. The syphilis
jokes, the danger of "drinking after" a friend, Mrs. Overdone's ruined eyes and her immersion in the "tub," the hangman and the bawd assistant, the dead criminal's clothes, even
that immense comic absurdity Barnardine, all live in an atmosphere of black comedy where the laughter is never allowed to dissipate into Gilbert and Sullivan. The "joke" always penetrates. Pompey's assimilation of the death house to
the brothel—there is a haunting air of macabre truth about
it. The play is totally improbable, but the implications of the
plot and characters are grimly real.

"Like doth quit like, and Measure still for Measure"
(V.1.412), says the Duke. The application of the text of Luke
to the play has a certain ironic twist to it. None of the actions, to which "measure for measure" is specifically applied,
is consummated. Claudio is not killed, Isabella is not rav-
ished, and Angelo is not executed. Even the punishment of
Pompey ends with a compromise which gives him a new job
in the death house. Barnardine is also, finally, not executed.
Furthermore, the nonconsummation is insisted on as a cau-
sative principle. As Claudio has *not* died, neither shall Angelo
be executed—on that count; as Isabella does not lose her virginity to him, he is not guilty of the "violation of sacred
chastity" and therefore free of that; Mariana is not to suffer
further her dismal half-spinsterhood half-widowhood—but

she has also not had to convince Angelo to acknowledge her as his wife. The application of measure for measure is all muted. Is it really pertinent, then, to think that as punishment matches crime, half-crime matches half-punishment? But then it is the Duke's interference which makes for the nonconsummation, and in most cases for the half-punishment too.

And do we in fact feel that the shrinking of the counter-measure has blotted out the impetus of the original act or contingency? The original mental suffering is real. It is only the issue of it into action which is missing. Claudio suffers acutely under the charge of his criminality because he has involved his girl and himself. He suffers even more under the terror of death, because it forces on him the humiliation of finding out his cowardice. Isabella suffers under the horrible choice between the violation of her sexuality and the proper affection for her brother. Angelo suffers in discovering what a scoundrel he is, and then living under the threat of a public discovery and the seeming actuality of condemnation. The irony of the measure-for-measure principle (so clearly enunciated by the Duke) is that in the play, contrariwise, it does not matter much what happens, but what your thoughts were when you tried to do the act, and what your thoughts were when you believed that something would happen to you as a result. The play turns, not on the acts to which "measure for measure" pointedly refers in detail, but to the thoughts behind the acts and the characters behind the thoughts.

Not only are we made to look at the skillful jugglery of the pieces across the board so that justice is done "and measure still for measure." We are made to see in the latter half of the play a kind of mental life in the characters which in its simplicity and unquestioningness is very similar to the actions they perform. Everyone has noticed the peculiarity of Isabella's readiness to fall in with the Mariana strategem, without so much as a comment. Everyone has noticed the silence of Isabella (is it acceptance or not?) at the Duke's reference to *their* marriage. Everyone has observed the want of explanation by Mariana of the substitution play. In the second part of this piece, the characters are deliberately blooded of their superfluous vitality which enabled them to entertain potentially two ideas—contradictory ideas—at once, and have eloquence for whichever one came uppermost—as Claudio when first he listens to the Duke, and second when he faces the possibility of escaping death. Or Juliet listening appreciatively to the Duke's moral mongering ("I take the shame with joy" [*MM* II.3.36]) and then altering when confronted with the death of her lover.

> O injurious love
> That respites me a life whose very comfort
> Is still a dying horror
>
> (*MM* II.3.40)

In the second part one has people totally subject to the impulse of a single idea, much too clearly and simply conceived, and the ideas themselves dominate the comedy of what is done with them.[2]

Such ideas, for instance, as similarity, equivalence, and substitution. The Duke cavalierly suggests to the Provost that he substitute Barnardine's head for Claudio's, and waves away any notion that Angelo would know the difference with the remark, "Death is a great disguiser." However, Raguzine dies ("a notorious pirate" who doubtless merited to die, and died very conveniently), and his head saves Barnardine's. Mariana is swapped for Isabella at the crucial moment. No one can seriously maintain that these two instances are anything except enormous jokes on the legal notion of equivalence. But there is almost as suggestive an ironic pattern in similar past actions with widely different social values. Procuring is a crime. As poor Pompey aptly agrees, "Indeed, it does stink in some sort" (*MM* III.2.29). But he also aptly characterizes it as lawful—"if the law would allow it" (*MM* III.1.227). Apparently at times the law does. Certainly neither the Duke nor Isabella sees anything wrong with their making arrangements for Mariana's sleeping with Angelo. If Mariana had any doubts (which we are not allowed to believe), they are laid to rest by the Duke's bland assurance, "He is your husband on a *pre-contract*" (*MM* IV.1.71). But this legal fiction apparently did not save Juliet (and Claudio) from the Duke's censure, though the terms in which Claudio describes his relations with Juliet are so startlingly similar that we are forced to notice it:

> Upon a true *contract*
> I got possession of Julietta's bed.
> You know the lady; she is fast my wife
> Save that we do the denunciation lack
> Of outward order.
>
> (*MM* I.2.145)

The Duke's own position on this is clearly expressed when he informs Juliet that it was exactly her being in love with her lover which made her act "most offenseful" (*MM* II.3.26), and merits its denunciation as a piece of immorality. That Angelo is deceived into his act of immorality does not matter, but that Juliet wanted to sleep with Claudio does.

The suggestion of the play to us is overwhelmingly this: the real tests of Claudio, Juliet, Isabella, Angelo, are all men-

tal. Their real sufferings are all mental. The acts of the Duke
when he prevents the full measure of evil (as when he substitutes Mariana for Isabella, or induces the Provost to refrain
from executing Claudio) are a special form of a puppet show.
We are meant to contrast this puppetry with the world of the
first three acts where everyone except the Duke sees and feels
the consequences of a plot set on a collision course. The
Duke, as with a stopwatch, halts the consequences and re-
adjusts the outcome. This is not just tragicomedy where
unpleasantness is suspended in favor of a gentler comic denouement. The solution (here the Duke's) is itself an ironic
commentary on the nature of the real world. The "satisfactory" comedy is deliberately at variance with the feelings of
the real world.

The tone and color of *Measure for Measure* is highly ironic
comedy. The people are real, for part of the play at least (the
first three acts), and show up the stupidity and barbarity of
what is happening to them. This stupidity and barbarity is
connected with legal processes. It is the law, as it normally is
seen in process. If one has a strict lawgiver, what more likely
(especially in comedy) than that he is a hypocrite? And who
would be caught in the stricter interpretation of the law but
the least guilty? If one sees the law applied, what would one
expect to find but a constable like Elbow—whose glorious
function, moreover, is to introduce us to pregnant malaprop-
isms such as characterizing the judge as a malefactor and the
criminal as benefactor? If one finds a "good" administrator
like Escalus or the Provost, what will this goodness consist
in except common sense and good nature which prevent him
from doing anything directly stupid?

We are asked to look at a reform situation—and again we
are prepared to find that the reform goes all wrong. Comedies naturally are against the *unco guid* and the very idea of

reform is a fair subject for joking, since the root of comedy is the notion of a stable human nature, and those who try to change it are either fools or knaves.

But it is here that we reach our complication. For allowing for the expected wickedness of the reforming administrator, and the absurdities of his reforms, we are confronted by another reformer, and this time a sort of play producer who operates behind the scenes reversing Angelo's evil, but also producing a shadow play of his own in which the issues of law, the tests of morality, above all the probing of self, have the leading interest. At the same time the complexity of the characters is thinned out and the issues come to the fore. But we are now made to wonder about the Duke himself, apart from either his change in the outcome or his manipulation of the characters. What is he up to, what does he know, what sort of person are we to take him to be?

The key is perhaps partly in the relationship of this sort of stage management and shadow play to the law—seen in actual human situations. Both the play and the process of law involve simplification in management, and the manager in this case is the Duke. He sometimes looks a little like Prospero, who also controls almost everything that happens in *The Tempest*. Prospero is explicitly a stage manager. Both the storm which brings his enemies into his power and the masque which he puts on for the terror of the shipwrecked, and for the amusement and the instruction of Ferdinand and Miranda, are achieved by the same spirits, now as agents, now as actors. His magic is the source of power in either instance.[3]

Our Duke does not have magic—for his is superficially an ordinary sort of world rather than an Enchanted Island. He also never puts on what are literally plays. But instead of magic he has an enhanced power of penetration ("When I perceive your Grace, like pow'r Divine / hath looked upon my passes" [*MM* V.1.369]), and the luckiest possible knack of being everywhere at the right moment—which will stand him in as good a stead. And instead of putting on plays, he uses the model of the stage—the happy ending, the villains comparatively mildly punished, the "proper" marriages—for the outcome of his comedy. And with it go the simplification of character and action of such comedies. The Duke is also a reformer, in the deepest sense of the word, one who not only tries to make better a bad situation in Vienna but tries to probe and illustrate the meaning of law in society. What is intriguing is that when one sees the complications of the real world in the first part of the play become the subject of the Duke's reforms, the action and characters are immediately headed, formally at least, for the lightest of light comedy.

Not quite, however. For now the stage manager becomes human, and by all sorts of hints we are made to put exactly the wrong questions (in our own minds) about the actions and characters—so that one wonders about the Duke's wisdom, his integrity, and most serious in a comedy, his sense of humor.

What is gained by deceiving Isabella into pleading for Angelo's life?

> But I will keep her ignorant of her good
> to make her heavenly comforts of despair
> (*MM* IV.3.109)

says the Duke. Does she attain these comforts? Or does her moral status improve in our eyes when she pleads for Angelo on the legal grounds that he only thought he committed the crime whereas her brother actually did so? Of course not.

Here is our old friend Isabella, with exactly the same mentality she showed earlier. But there is an addition:

> I partly think
> A due sincerity governed his deeds
> Till he did look on me. Since it is so,
> Let him not die.
>
> (*MM* V. 1.446)

Is this one of our hints showing the real, complicated story still alive under the surface?

Isabella and, earlier, Juliet are the subjects of the Duke's moral improvement: Mariana is there to have her happiness restored. But what of Lucio, who in the course of the play merits only punishment and the payment of retribution? Lucio is one of the troublers of the understanding in this enigmatic comedy. He and Barnardine keep moving from farcical existence into something like a more ordinary dimension of reality, and jolting us as they do so. As a friend he very sensibly gingers up Isabella's approach to the deputy; as a hard-hearted ex-customer he deserts poor old Pompey in his hour of need. In his encounter with the Duke one sees an entirely new side of him—his power of imaginative fantasy. The story of the Duke's fictitious lechery is magnificently equipped with detail. The beggar with the garlic breath, the clack dish for money contributions, the horribly convincing absurdity of the dignified, self-examining Duke reduced to sordid and ridiculous sexual situations—it all adds up. Not to truth, of course, but Lucio's interesting imagination generates a certain shakiness in our straightforward belief in the Duke himself; at moments, it seems, madly, unlikely that Lucio could have invented *everything* in the story. It also fits with the Duke's rage at Lucio, his serious complaint that when you are in authority you cannot control what people think of you and say of you. They will fill in a picture of you that accords with what they want to believe must be the interesting human reality—and this can cover a lot of territory. The Duke finds it exasperating that he cannot prevent himself being described as a drunkard and lecher. He resents as much that he is described as a "very superficial ignorant unweighing fellow."

The sovereign in disguise, moving among his undiscerning subjects and listening to their censures is a familiar comedy subject. Shakespeare himself used it in *Henry V* where the king talks familiarly (and unknown) with his soldiers on the night before Agincourt. This situation seems usually to demand that the disguised sovereign, when finally revealed, gives only token punishment for the abuse he has sustained incognito and eventually fills the cap with gold pieces. Not so the Duke with Lucio. Whether one agrees with Lucio's comic description of marriage with a whore as "pressing to death, whipping, and hanging" (*MM* V.1.522), it is certainly the punishment, slight or severe, which sticks in our minds. *Noblesse oblige* is a maxim which does not apply much to the Duke. And Lucio's account—the account of the bastard child—and the general meanness of Lucio's conduct also put the episode uncomfortably inside a realistic setting. But the Duke doesn't escape. In this action he is small-minded and pompous.

And surely we have a moment of indignation about his unthinking readiness to do away with Barnardine, when he apparently recollects nothing of that magnificent character. We must not forget that we have the Provost and not the Duke to thank for Barnardine's survival in the first place. And surely also when Barnardine has filled us with laughter with his refusal to "rise and be hang'd" because he is not in a state of grace and "will not die today for any man's persuasion" (*MM* IV.3.65), the Duke's rejoinder "Unfit to live or die, . . . O gravel heart / After him, fellows, bring him to the block!" (*MM* IV.3.71) leaves us with a dislike for his outraging of our comic susceptibilities. At this point he is much too real to be accepted as Shakespeare's Red Queen in Alice's Vienna. Indeed suddenly, as in the case of Lucio, he steps right out of that comedy role in Vienna, the *deus ex machina* of benevolent intent, and shows his face as a vindictive, complacent, and insensitive bore.[4]

The play is a composition of two pieces, with two joined but different themes. First it is about the law and about reform (legal reform) of a society. That which is about law deals most specifically with the inadequacy of law with respect to truth—truth being defined as the meaning of the total experience of an individual in a given situation which calls for the intervention of the law. The Duke says that his experimental retirement from Vienna will show: "If power change purpose, what our seemers be" (*MM* I.3.54)—he certainly refers to Angelo. But it not only shows up Angelo. The pressure of the circumstances shows the contrast of seeming and depth in Claudio, Juliet, Isabella. Angelo was probably a convinced ascetic until his special temptation came along. But when it does come, it finds someone with violent sexual passion only to be satisfied by a truly perverse experience—violation of a nun, and flavoring that piece of sexuality by the threat of and delight in torturing her brother. Isabella has the proper horror of trading her virginity for her brother's life. But when she bursts into hysterical rage against him so savagely as to wish for his death and professes willingness to bring it about, we are entitled to wonder about the quality of the original virtue. The Isabella who seeks for greater restraint on the nuns of St. Clare, and the Isabella who fears about Claudio "Lest thou a feverous life shouldst entertain / and six or seven winters more respect / than a perpetual honour" (*MM* III.1.74) (at about twenty-two) illuminates the Isabella of immature priggishness and total moral blindness. Both Angelo and Isabella do not know themselves—to quote Escalus's description of the Duke's leading passion. Nor does Claudio; he does not, before this, know himself for a coward.

Throughout this part of the play there is a formal requirement of law (the punishment of deeds) which is backed by a "proper" interpretation of virtue and vice, life and death, and religion. None of this structure stands up under pressure. The Duke's philosophy is convincing to Claudio until death is a reality. The Duke's morality seems such to Juliet until her lover's death is an actuality. Angelo is pious—until his piety and virtue are conjoined with power to be otherwise. Isabella is a pleader for forgiveness for her brother, and gallant in offering herself to hypothetical scourging and death—until the price to be paid is sexual sacrifice. Everybody is a seemer until the moment of truth comes. Angelo and Isabella are made to show their deeper (and worse) selves; Juliet her better; Claudio an ordinary, not very dignified human self, which merits, at the least, toleration.

To this part of the play the appropriateness of "Judge not lest ye be judged" is obvious. The confusion which can exist between the thief and the judge on the bench is a sound reason for honesty to be pretty modest in its claims. The example of the application of law—at the high level to Claudio and at the low level to Pompey and Froth—is wonderfully funny. It is hardly intended to reassure one that law in process will be better than in theory. The good judges, like Escalus, are people who for the most part do nothing, or nothing until the situation grows aggravated, as when Pompey's renewed activity lands him in jail. It is clear that Escalus would not have revived the statute, long a dead letter, anyway. When it is revived, he does as little as he decently can to enforce it.

Which brings us to the second topic—reform. Under what conditions does reform occur in our play, and what are the results of the reform instituted? Reform occurs when someone—the ruler—has not been doing his job. That job appears to be a fatherly interference when license becomes scandalous. This is rather vaguely defined. Obviously what Angelo does is a mistake. Perhaps it was also a mistake for the Duke to allow him to initiate it. It is extremely difficult to make a case for the play as a piece where everyone is improved morally by his and her experience. Angelo's experiment does not succeed—as far as we can see. The wise burgers have already decreed that the brothels in the city should stand "for seed" (*MM* I.2.98). The Duke, in the last part of the play, makes no arrangements for continuing the campaign Angelo started. He is only concerned at undoing the particular harms which resulted from Angelo's policy. As far as we know, Vienna relapsed into its condition of easy depravity, unmolested. It is, the atmosphere of the play suggests, the more ordinary condition. It is punctuated at times by its extreme opposite (is this another case of the rats seeking "their proper bane"?); but there is no mention of a balanced or more balanced condition resulting from the two extremes.

In the second place, there is something extremely pointed in the picture of the reformer. He is someone "who above all other strifes, contended to know himself" and is happier to see others merry than to be merry himself. This sounds well, in the mouth of Escalus, until one reflects that it also describes a person who is quite certain he can know himself, and someone who derives his main interest from other people's concerns. This exactly fits the Duke. He is, I am inclined to think, no less satirized, though in a gentler vein, than any other of the actively moral persons in this play. His stagemanship ignores the complex reality of other people's lives. In some instances, as in Barnardine, he is prepared to ignore the matter of the life altogether when one needs a substitute head. He is most efficient at programming moral tests for the improvement of his subjects, but as we see there is always a certain uncomfortable aspect of these tests. He wants, in fact, to make them better people, other people. When Lucio tries the same trick on him, and in defiance of the facts creates a lecherous, drunken, frivolous Duke, the old fantastical Duke of dark corners, he is outraged. Are we being asked perhaps to compare the two kinds of mental activity? The Duke, in *Measure for Measure* anyway, did not reform Vienna; perhaps it was all done to show up Angelo. But it does more than that. In the combination of the lighthearted comedy and caricature, there are barbs about the humanity of the Duke himself and his reforming zeal. Perhaps he and Isabella are well matched. In any case the marriage will probably give him something else to think about. I doubt if he tried to reform Vienna again.

Conclusion

The scene between Brutus and Cassius and the rest of the conspirators, after the murder of Caesar, is the most suggestive evidence for the different threads of argument in this book (*JC* III.1.106). The bathing of the hands and swords in blood is the completion of the significance of the murder. As the conspirators think of future dramatic reenactments of their deed, they see a continuous link between the original murder and its immortality—and that immortality comes through the theater.

But, in Brutus's words on this, there is, momentarily, a denigration of the future dramatic display in comparison with the here-and-now unique event. The contrast is between Caesar's future bleeding in "sport" and the body "who now on Pompey's basis lies along, / no worthier than the dust." Yet Shakespeare reserves for the conspirators an immortality of the same mistake that now possesses them. They believe that they have won liberty for their state, and have been liberty's champions. But the history that follows, in the rest of *Caesar* and *Antony and Cleopatra,* proves them wrong. The emergence of another tyranny is what actually happened. The liberty which is to be the theme song of the original scene has been permanently lost, at least as far as Rome is concerned.

Yet perhaps exactly in this, the discrepancy between the

historical result and the dramatic performance of the artistic fiction lies something that the play asserts. There *is* a love of liberty in Brutus, there is a resentment of domination by a single man. These sentiments did not win in Rome in the last century before Christ; perhaps they never have or never will, says Shakespeare. But they are among the great permanent aspirations of mankind, and as such belong in enlargement of the historical deed and its "meaning," *sub specie aeternitatis.* This is the area where the theater exploits our imagination of the historical potential, as distinct from the historical fact. This imagination is also tied to the physical presence of the actor of Caesar miming death and humiliation, and that of the actor of Brutus miming conviction of permanent victory. From these actors' presentation—and of course from the way that earlier in the play they have read the parts of the two men—emerges the ambiguous versatility of the truth that survives. It is held in check only by the broad inhibition of the text as interpreted by the director. So the event in its factual uniqueness still lives, in relation to the changing bodies, voices, and gestures of each new generation of actors, as they create for us the impression of personality for the two parts.

The combination of language and physical presence is at its strongest in poetic drama, and perhaps strongest of all in Shakespeare. This combination lures the professional actor to the enrichment of his own relation to the audience in the theater before him, while he plays to his fellow actors on the stage. This condition moves the play beyond the definition of the character's role and the event's probability or convincingness to a response only partly analyzable, haunted by echoes verbal and passionate, of things half-known and half-heard. This is actor's country; it is explored psychologically in person by Richard II, and Antony, by Falstaff and Hotspur, by Brutus and Coriolanus. This actor's country itself is the raw material in *Measure for Measure,* as we ask ourselves with what kind of reality that play mocks us or gives us a glimpse of a new verity.

Beyond Shakespeare's version of the inspired amateur actors, like Richard II and the others, and their struggle between their histrionic longing and their efficiency, beyond the play-within-the-play's ambiguous demand on our sympathy in *Measure for Measure,* there runs a continuous suggestion of the independence, partial at least, of actor's language, actor's poetry, from the total integration with character or action. These fascinate us in their own right—because the poetry, as it blends with the voice and the gesture, hints at a new color that suffuses a new reality, of which the theater is the image.

Notes

Chapter 1

1. See Janet Adelman, *The Common Liar: An Essay on* Antony and Cleopatra, Yale University Press, New Haven and London, 1973, p.141. "We are asked to accept a play with too many short scenes and too many minor characters, with passions generally in excess of their objects and characters who claim to be larger than life: a play which gives us the whole world and then demands that we exchange it for a kiss. We cannot measure this play by any ordinary scale: it violates every principle of classical decorum and establishes a new decorum of its own. . . . [U]ltimately we must take it on its own terms, like the crocodile."

2. Traversi has a nice sense of the necessary combination of elements here. "[J]ust as earth and slime can be quickened into life, briefly and elusively indeed, but none the less truly, by the action upon them of fire and air, so the very elements of waste and vanity which nurtured this tragedy have become, by the time it reaches its necessary conclusion, constituent ingredients in the creation of an intuition of immortality." Derek Traversi, *Shakespeare: The Roman Plays,* Stanford University Press, Stanford, California, 1963.

3. These weaknesses, of course, must be present and emphasized. As Adelman notes, the skeptics are allowed their full say in this play, and Cleopatra herself gives the most skeptical view with her "boy my greatness" speech. Without this persistent questioning, the imaginative affirmations could not emerge triumphant (p. 110). "In this play, the naysayers may have reason and justice on their side; but as Plato suspected when he banished poetry from his republic, reason and justice are no match for poetry" (p. 104).

4. Traversi's comment on the effect of death at the end of this process is

interesting. "The whole development of the play has moved consistently towards this point. . . . [D]eath, which had seemed to be in Shakespeare's early tragedies incontrovertible evidence of the subjection of love and human values to time, has now become an instrument of release, the necessary condition of an experience which, though dependent upon circumstance is, by virtue of its intensity and by the intimations of *value* which accompany even its more dubious manifestations, in some sense incommensurate with them—that is, even in its stressed weaknesses, capable of a glimpse of 'immortality.'" Traversi, *Roman Plays,* pp. 202–3.

5. As Adelman, *The Common Liar,* has well noted, "*Antony and Cleopatra* constantly insists on its status as a play; characters stage emotions and accuse one another of bad acting; the pattern of framing suggests that we see the central figures as actors in a play within the play" (p. 39). I shall have more to say about this emphasis on the theatrical medium at the end of this chapter.

6. As usual, Adelman puts this nicely when she says that the hyperbole associated with Antony, like all hyperbole, presents the spectacle of man making his own imaginative universe in despite of all reality. Adelman, *The Common Liar,* p. 115.

7. Traversi has a good ear for Shakespearean politicians. Of Augustus's marriage arrangement he says, ". . . we need not interpret it as consciously insincere—for such as Caesar are so convinced of their rectitude that the need for insincerity does not occur to them." *Roman Plays,* p. 128. See also pp. 135–37.

Those who are interested in Anne Righter's views of Shakespeare and the idea of the theater must deal with her claims about *Antony and Cleopatra.* She finds that in this play, "the play metaphor continues to express emptiness and deceit" (p. 187). She cites Caesar's disapproval at II.7.122 in support of her claim that Shakespeare in this tragedy degrades shadows, dreams, actors, and the play. Anne Righter, *Shakespeare and the Idea of the Play,* Barnes & Noble, New York, 1963, p. 188. One must ask whether Ms. Righter is correct in hearing Shakespeare's voice in Caesar's values or whether, rather, Traversi is closer.

Traversi puts the opposition to Righter quite well in his description of act V. "Everything that is to follow is based, in a very relevant sense, upon illusion, upon the determined exclusion of reality which has from the first been implied in the tragic relationship which has now found in death its natural and appropriate conclusion; but the illusion is after all itself a manifestation of life and, as such, capable of genuine tragic significance. Whilst admitting at each stage the presence of the other, more desolate realities, we need not impose upon an experience the poetic expression of which guarantees its value a unilateral moral interpretation which belongs to, but does not exhaust, the meaning of the play" (p. 191).

8. So Philip Edwards, in a phrase characteristically brief and apt, finds this partly a tragedy "of the ousting of the old richness and generosity by the colourless efficiency of youth." *Shakespeare and the Confines of Art.* Methuen, London; Barnes & Noble, New York, 1968, p. 121.

9. Adelman notes that Antony refers to Aeneas and Dido, and that Aeneas's fruitful Roman marriage to Lavinia has been "replaced" by Antony's disastrous one to Octavia. The values of the *Aeneid* are political, spatial, and temporal; those in *Antony and Cleopatra* the values of love and the nonspatial and nontemporal. Adelman, *The Common Liar,* p. 73.

10. This is very nearly what Adelman describes in saying that in tragedy poetry is usually at the service of action; in the romances, action is usually at the service of poetry, but in *Antony and Cleopatra* poetry and action conflict, each making its own assertions and having its own validity. Adelman, *The Common Liar,* pp. 167–68.

Chapter 2

1. Although Anne Righter has closely studied the theatrical elements in *Richard II,* she finds the association of royalty with acting totally negative. See her discussion in *Shakespeare and the Idea of the Play,* pp. 122–27.

2. Philip Edwards, British Academy Lectures, 1970.

3. Ibid.

4. This is precisely what Derek Traversi has in mind when he says that Richard is "sincere and yet engaged in acting his own sincerity, possessed of true feeling and elaborately artificial in expressing it." *Shakespeare from Richard II to Henry V,* Stanford University Press, Stanford, California, 1957, p. 40.

5. As Traversi puts it, Richard's "sentiments flow . . . into poetic forms at once powerful enough to move and superficial, conventional enough, to induce a suspension of complete acceptance." *Shakespeare: The Roman Plays,* p. 29.

6. Theodore Weiss shares this view of the deposition scene. He says that

only in this sense does Richard "turn up an occasion adequate to his histrionic powers. . . . As a king he was not too convincing an actor; only as an actor, we may say, has he become a king." *The Breath of Clowns and Kings: Shakespeare's Early Comedies and Histories,* Atheneum, New York, 1971, p. 245.

7. W. B. Yeats, in "At Stratford on Avon," *Essays and Introductions,* Macmillan, New York, 1961, p. 108.

8. For the importance of this exchange between Gaunt and Bolingbroke for the play's exploration of the conflict between reality and the power of language, see Traversi, *Shakespeare from Richard II to Henry V,* p. 18, and more especially, Weiss, *The Breath of Clowns and Kings,* pp. 216–18. As Weiss points out, Gaunt shows he is aware both of the powers of language and of its limits in the face of reality.

9. Weiss has this in mind when he contrasts the man of action to the poet. He says, ". . . the extent to which dream and action often part company, the way in which absorption in the subjective correlative can eclipse the world at large, *Richard II* is a triumphant enactment of this dilemma." *The Breath of Clowns and Kings,* p. 258.

10. Traversi has seen this delicate balance. "The judgment which Richard's words prompt in us is not, indeed, to be simply made." *Shakespeare from Richard II to Henry V,* p. 30. See also pages 4 and 9 for discussions of the complexity in respectively evaluating Richard and Henry.

11. Weiss says, "Thus we can plot the play in terms of words alone. It moves from its early encomium to language delivered by Mowbray and others, fitting while Richard is still in charge; to Richard's regime of words; to Richard's final admission of language's inadequacy in itself. Those exiled from their language 'die'; those living only in language, no less exiled from experience and reality or their 'mother earth' . . . also 'die'. Yet, having driven language as far as it can go and turning from it to that only pure utterance, music, finding both insufficient, Richard breaks through. Paradoxically enough, the word in its extremity becomes deed, his last heroic action, or the bridge to tragedy. When poetry or language becomes self-infatuated, brings catastrophe down upon itself, it shows itself able, if only in the last moment, to rise to the splendidly dramatic and heroic." *The Breath of Clowns and Kings,* p. 258.

12. See John Neville Figgis, *The Divine Right of Kings,* Introduction by G. R. Elton, Harper Textbooks, 1965.

13. W. B. Yeats, in "The Tragic Theatre," *Essays and Introductions,* p. 243.

Chapter 3

1. James Winny, *The Player King,* Barnes & Noble, New York, 1968.

2. *The First Part of the History of Henry IV,* ed. J. Dover Wilson, Cambridge, 1946, pp. vii–xiii.

3. Ibid., p. 1.

4. ". . . though both Hotspur and Falstaff are first rate poets, similar in their proclivity to pungent terms and images and to plain dealing, they are finally and fundamentally as opposite as their names suggest." Weiss, *The Breath of Clowns and Kings,* p. 283.

5. As Weiss says, "Tangy words and all, he never for a moment recognizes what a poet he is, especially since his contempt for poetry is based on a most limited notion of it." *The Breath of Clowns and Kings,* p. 280.

6. Dover Wilson, *Henry IV,* pp. xxi–xxii.

7. Ibid., p. xxii.

8. See especially "The Choice and the Balance," in *The Fortunes of Falstaff,* MacMillan, Cambridge, 1944, pp. 114–28.

9. *King Henry V,* ed. J. Dover Wilson, Cambridge, 1947; see especially "Introduction," pp. vii–xlviii.

10. Robert Ornstein, *A Kingdom for a Stage: The Achievement of Shakespeare's History Plays,* Harvard University Press, Cambridge, Massachusetts, 1972): ". . . has an excellent discussion of the complexity of Henry's character. For example, he notes that Henry is the only member of his council to grasp the moral issue and the horror of war" (p. 181). "Yet rather than grieving over the fates of his soldiers and war widows and orphans, he seems more agonized at the thought 'that he will be accountable for all this suffering'" (p. 194).

11. Traversi has a more balanced view. Thus his comment on act II, scene 2: "This scene would be sufficient to prove, were proof necessary, that it would be wrong to suppose that Shakespeare, in portraying Henry, intends to stress the note of hypocrisy. Its effect is rather to bring out certain contradictions, moral and human, inherent in the notion of a successful king." *Shakespeare from Richard II to Henry V,* p. 177.

Chapter 4

1. J. P. Kenyon, *The Stuarts: A Study in English Kingship,* Science Editions, John Wiley and Sons, New York, 1967, p. 111.

2. This is one of the closest links between the chronicle plays and the Roman plays. As Derek Traversi notes, the chronicle plays hinted "at the presence of certain stresses upon the figure of the monarch, at the sacrifice of common human qualities involved in the almost inhuman impersonality required by the royal office," *Shakespeare from Richard II to Henry V*, pp. 16–17. This should be coupled with another remark of Travaersi's on *Antony and Cleopatra:*

> The human and political elements of the tragedy are constantly balanced one against the other. In the political order Octavius prevails, and we would not have it otherwise. In a somewhat similar way the Lancastrian ideal had prevailed in the *Henry IV* plays and had been confirmed by national triumph in *Henry V.* In neither case are we left in doubt that it must be so, that the defeat of the principle of authority and ordered rule would have meant ruin for the universal empire of Rome, just as that of Henry IV or his son by their enemies would have brought riot and misrule to England. Order is, in fact, a necessary, an indispensable good; but it is affirmed, in the political sphere, through a choice that involves the rejection, as incompatible, of certain possibilities of life. From this point of view, and without seeking to minimize the enormous differences that separate them, the rejection of Falstaff and the death of Cleopatra share a common tragic implication.

D. Traversi, *Shakespeare: The Roman Plays*, p. 13.

Chapter 5

1. Plutarch's "Life of Brutus."
2. In regard to Brutus's theoretical idealism, Traversi cites Brutus's lines,

> For let the gods so speed me as I love
> The name of honor more than I fear death.
>
> (I.2.88)

and comments, "It will be, perhaps, one of the lessons of Brutus' tragedy that the 'names' of things, however noble and consoling in abstraction, are no substitute for a balanced consideration of their reality." *Shakespeare: The Roman Plays*, p. 25.

3. See Philip Edwards, British Academy Lectures, pp. 7–8.

4. Of the brilliant performance of Sir Ralph Richardson, suffering from a stroke and exploiting the infirmity in *No Man's Land* by Harold Pinter.

Chapter 6

1. See the *New Cambridge Edition* (1922), p. 113. In "Some Composite Scenes in *Measure for Measure,*" *Shakespeare Quarterly* 15, no. 1 (1964), pp. pp. 67–74, S. Musgrove looks at the difficulties posed by Wilson and discusses them in terms of changes in the composition as Shakespeare's conception of the play changed.

2. The different nature of the play's two halves is frequently noted, usually with dissatisfaction expressed over the second half, implying that Shakespeare would have done a better job had he spent more time or been less constrained by his sources. See Mary Lascelles, *Shakespeare's Measure for Measure* (London, 1953), p. 89. Also, E. M. W. Tillyard, *Shakespeare's Problem Plays* (London, 1950), pp. 123, 129. Even L. C. Knights in "The Ambiguity of *Measure for Measure,*" *Scrutiny* 10 (1942), p. 232, sees in the last two acts obvious signs of haste and little more than a drawing out and resolution of the plot. However, F. R. Leavis in his reply to Knights, "The Greatness of *Measure for Measure,*" *Scrutiny* 10 (1942), pp. 243–45, finds each touch in the second half significant and asserts that it is a skillful masterpiece of economy. W. W. Lawrence in *"Measure for Measure* and Lucio,*" *Shakespeare Quarterly* 9 (1958), pp. 443–55, outlines some possible positive reasons for the change.

3. See G. Wilson Knight, *"Measure for Measure* and the Gospels,*" *The Wheel of Fire* (London: Methuen, 1930; 4th rev. ed., 1949), p. 79.

4. In "The Mood of *Measure for Measure,*" *Shakespeare Quarterly* 14 (1963), pp. 31–38, D. C. Marsh traces what he feels are subtle digs at the Duke's character throughout the play. Also see F. R. Leavis, "The Greatness of *Measure for Measure,*" pp. 234–35, 238–39, for criticisms of the Duke built into the play. Leavis finds the Duke's attitude toward death especially telling.

Index